Preserving Made Easy

Preserving
Made Easy

ELLIE TOPP & MARGARET HOWARD

FIREFLY BOOKS

A FIREFLY BOOK

Published by Firefly Books Ltd. 2012

Copyright © 2012 Firefly Books Ltd.
Text copyright © 2012 Eleanor Topp and Margaret Howard

First printing

Publisher Cataloging-in-Publication Data (U.S.)
Topp, Ellie.
Preserving made easy : small batches & simple techniques / Ellie Topp and Margaret Howard.
[320] p. : col. ill. ; cm.
Includes index.
Summary: Step-by-step, easy to follow techniques and recipes for preserving jams, conserves, pickles, salsas, marinades, flavored oils and more.
ISBN-13: 978-1-77085-094-1 (pbk.)
1. Canning and preserving. 2. Fruit -- Preservation. 3. Vegetables -- Preservation.
I. Howard, Margaret, 1930- . II. Title.
641.814   dc23   TX603.T65 2012

Library and Archives Canada Cataloguing in Publication
Topp, Ellie, 1938-
Preserving made easy : small batches & simple techniques / Ellie Topp, Margaret Howard.
Includes index.
ISBN-13: 978-1-77085-094-1
1. Canning and preserving. 2. Cookbooks.
I. Howard, Margaret, 1930- II. Title.
TX603.T653 2012   641.4'2   C2012-901467-2

Published in the United States by
Firefly Books (U.S.) Inc.
P.O. Box 1338, Ellicott Station
Buffalo, New York 14205

Published in Canada by
Firefly Books Ltd.
66 Leek Crescent
Richmond Hill, Ontario L4B 1H1

Cover and interior design: Christine Rae

Printed in China

The publisher gratefully acknowledges the financial support for our publishing program by the Government of Canada through the Canada Book Fund as administered by the Department of Canadian Heritage.

Photo credits

Page 48: Shutterstock: Sever180, Karl Allgaeuer, oksix, CCat82, Larina Natalia, Kachalkina Veronika. Page 80: Shutterstock: Yana Gayvoronskaya, HLPhoto, Madien, Boris Bulychev, Markus Mainka, Madien. Page 128: Shutterstock: Elitsa Lambova, Forster Forest, Forster Forest, Zhukov Oleg, Bernardin, Anne Gardon. Page 160: Bernardin, Lilyana Vynogradova, Bernardin, David P. Smith, Juriah Mosin, S. Duffet. Page 208: Bernardin, Anne Gordon, Anna Subbotina, Lilyana Vynogradova. Page 240: Dirk Ott, Bernardin, Africa Studio, Yana Gayvoronskaya.

Contents

Preserving Made Easy

MULTI-HUED PEPPERS, juicy peaches and nectarines, glowing red and purple grapes—all these delicious fruits beckon to us at the farmer's market or produce counter. We load our shopping baskets with this bounty from all over the world. And then what? We certainly enjoy eating the fresh produce. But deep within most of us lurks a desire to preserve these flavors for future enjoyment.

Many of us remember our grandmothers spending long hours in the summer preserving the produce from their large gardens. While few of us have a desire to return to the era of preserving large quantities of food for the cold months, we are developing a taste for new flavors and want to use them to enhance an otherwise simple meal. A flavorful bit of chutney, a rich salsa, a crisp pickle, a special sauce, or a flavored oil or vinegar adds interest to a meal while fitting a healthy lifestyle. Jams, conserves, marmalades and jellies can be spread on toast, English muffins or tea biscuits with no added butter necessary.

Throughout this book we offer recipes for smaller rather than larger finished amounts. A small yield gives more opportunity to make several different preserves. It also reduces the risk of scorching that is always a danger when cooking larger batches. And it makes large storage areas unnecessary. Most recipes can be made year round and, most important, at your convenience.

Preserving food is great fun and not at all difficult. When you decide to preserve food, there are two important things you must do. The first is to destroy all micro-organisms such as bacteria, molds and yeasts naturally present in food to prevent them from spoiling the preserved product. Having done this, the second thing is to make sure your preserving containers are sealed in such a way that other organisms cannot enter, otherwise they will cause your carefully prepared food to spoil.

Micro-organisms and enzymes naturally present in foods cause many changes to occur. Not all of these changes are bad. Many micro-organisms—bacteria, molds and yeasts—are intentionally used to create new forms of foods. For instance, bacteria added to milk produce creamy yogurt. Enzymes turn milk into curds, and molds introduced into the curds create wonderful cheeses. Wine-makers know the result of yeasts growing in grape juice. However, not all organisms cause changes that are desirable. They can cause food to spoil.

Today's methods of preserving are much easier, thanks to innovations from jar manufacturers. The two-piece closures, are much more foolproof than were the glass-topped sealer jars used in bygone days. And modern jars come in a variety of convenient sizes that let us preserve small amounts quickly without overwhelming our storage areas. The small batches featured in our book let you make a small amount of a tasty preserve in very short order.

We now have access to a wide variety of fruits and vegetables—some of which were unknown to North America until recently. Many of these fruits and vegetables, such as mangoes, papayas, fresh figs and even strawberries and a variety of peppers are now available year round. Almost all of our recipes can be made throughout the year with this greater availability. However, a few foods are only available for short times of the year. Seville oranges are a good example. They are usually in stores only in January and February. Other fruits and vegetables, although available throughout the year, may be of better quality at certain times. We believe the quality of our own locally grown produce is superior since it arrives fresh in our kitchens without extended storage. At other times, good imported produce is available—just remember, you may be paying more. Preserve when the quality is finest and price is lowest.

FOUR WAYS TO PRESERVE FOOD

Heat, acid, sugar and freezing are four common ways to prevent food from spoiling.

1. Heat

The easiest way to destroy micro-organisms present in food is to heat the food. Processing is the word traditionally used when filled jars of food are heated to specific temperatures for specific lengths of time. The times and temperatures required depend on the density of the food and the size of the jar.

All molds, yeasts and most bacteria are destroyed at the temperature of boiling water. However, some bacteria, such as *Clostridium botulinum*, can form spores that withstand very high temperatures. Therefore, although this bacteria is destroyed by boiling-water temperatures, its spores may survive. These spores develop into bacteria that are able to grow in an airtight environment (such as a canning jar) and produce a poisonous toxin causing botulism. Fortunately these bacteria cannot grow in the presence of acids such as vinegar or lemon juice.

2. Acid

For preserving purposes, food can be divided into two categories:

High-Acid Foods are sufficiently acidic to prevent the growth of any spores that survive boiling-water processing. Most fruits, some vegetables and some tomatoes are high-acid foods. They can be processed at the lower temperatures reached with a boiling-water canner.

Low-Acid Foods are not sufficiently acidic to inhibit the growth of bacteria spores that can survive boiling-water temperatures. The food must be preserved by processing in a pressure canner which reaches much higher temperatures than can be achieved with boiling-water methods. Pressure canning is used to process the canned foods we buy. In this book, we don't deal with pressure canning since few people have the equipment.

Fortunately, there are some low-acid foods that can be safely preserved at boiling-water temperatures by adding acid. This is the secret of pickling. If the acid in a food is strong enough, most micro-organisms cannot grow. Familiar acids used in this process are many types of vinegars and lemon juice. Thus, it is essential to measure the ingredients accurately and not alter either the amount of acid or the amount of vegetable.

A few micro-organisms are able to grow at high acid concentration. Therefore, it is now recommended that all pickled foods be processed in a boiling-water canner for short periods of time.

3. Sugar

Sugar present in high concentrations traps water in food, creating an environment where micro-organisms cannot grow. Jams and jellies are preserved in this way. Molds and some yeasts can grow on the surface of such foods, but only in the presence of air. An airtight seal achieved from heat processing prevents the growth of such molds and yeasts.

4. Freezing

Freezing stores food at such low temperatures that no micro-organism growth can occur. However, some enzyme activity can still go on in frozen vegetables, giving off-flavors. To prevent this, vegetables are generally blanched briefly before freezing. Fruits may be frozen in their raw state.

EQUIPMENT FOR SAFE BOILING-WATER PROCESSING

1. Boiling-Water Canner

A boiling-water canner is a large covered container generally made from steel- covered enamel or stainless steel. A rack fits inside to hold the jars, keeping them from touching one another and elevating them from the bottom of the canner to allow water to circulate freely around them. The canner must be deep enough to allow at least 1 inch (2.5 cm) of briskly boiling water to cover the filled jars and the diameter should be no more than 4 inches (10 cm) wider than the burner on the stove.

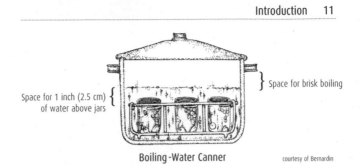

Space for 1 inch (2.5 cm) of water above jars

Space for brisk boiling

Boiling-Water Canner

courtesy of Bernardin

Any large cooking pot can be used for a canner as long as it has a tight-fitting lid and is large enough to hold the jars. A rack is essential for adequate circulation of water around the jars. A round cake rack can serve this purpose. If the rack does not have handles, you will need a jar lifter for removing the jars from the hot water.

2. Canning Jars and Lids

Before you start a recipe, be sure you have enough clean canning jars that are free from cracks or nicks. Canning jars, sometimes called mason jars, are designed to withstand the temperatures of boiling-water canning. They are available in a variety of shapes and sizes from small half-cup (125 mL) to large two-quart (2 L) jars. Our recipes are designed for small batches, so we generally use the 1 cup (250 mL) and 2 cup (500 mL) sizes.

Jars come in two sizes, standard and wide mouth. The standard size is most commonly used, but wide-mouthed jars are useful for packing foods in larger pieces, such as dill pickles. Lids are made in two pieces, a lid and a screw band to keep the lid in place. The lid has a sealing compound that allows it to form a seal with the jar. Each lid is used one time only to ensure a proper jar seal. The screw band can be reused.

A magnetic wand is very handy for lifting the lids from the hot water. Use a commercial one or glue a small magnet onto a piece of wooden dowel rod to make your own.

3. Essential Sweet Spread Equipment

A large saucepan is essential to allow the fruit mixture to come to a full rolling boil. It should be heavy to allow even distribution of heat and made of stainless steel or enamel to prevent reaction with the acid in the mixture. In our recipes, a "large saucepan" means one that holds approximately 4 quarts (4 L). A few of the larger recipes call for a "very large saucepan," meaning one that holds at least 6 quarts (6 L). Sweet spreads should be preserved in canning jars closed with a screw band and a new metal lid. It is best to use the smaller ½ cup (125 mL) or 1 cup (250 mL) canning jars because a breakdown of the gel may occur with the longer cooling time required for larger quantities. This results in a more liquid product.

You will also need a ladle or pitcher for putting the fruit mixture into jars. A wide-mouth funnel is also very helpful.

4. Essential Pickling Equipment

Most of the equipment needed for pickling is found in the usual well-equipped kitchen. You need a large stainless steel or enamel saucepan for cooking. Since most condiments are quite thick, a jar filler or wide-mouth funnel is very helpful for filling the jars. Canning jars and lids of any size can be used, but we like the 2 cup (500 mL) jars for pickles and the 1 cup (250 mL) jars for salsas, relishes and chutneys. The very small ½ cup (125 mL) jars are ideal for small amounts of savory sauces and for gift giving.

EASY STEP-BY-STEP PRESERVING

1. Food Selection and Preparation

The best preserves result from using the best ingredients. Use produce that is as fresh as possible and at the peak of quality. Most vegetables should be used as soon as possible, but some fruits may require further ripening. Many tender fruits are picked before they are fully ripe, so wait a day or so until their full flavor has developed. However, most fruits are best for preserving when they are slightly underripe.

Wash the food thoroughly to remove surface dirt and any traces of chemicals. Discard any bruised or moldy fruit since micro-organisms may have started to grow. Fruit with other surface blemishes or imperfections is fine to use. Next read through the recipe and set out the ingredients. Remember to measure accurately.

2. Equipment Preparation

For smaller jars (1 cup/250 mL), place jars in boiling-water canner. Add hot water to jars and canner until the water level reaches the top of the jars. For larger jars, add water to the jars and canner until the jars are about two-thirds full. Cover the canner and place over medium heat until the water is hot but not boiling. The jars do not need to be sterilized before processing, but they should be kept hot until they are filled. (Sterilization of the jars in boiling water is unnecessary as the boiling-water temperatures during the processing time will destroy any micro-organisms in the food as well as on the jars and lids.) If you live in an area with hard water, add a bit of vinegar to the water to prevent a film forming on the jars. It is helpful to have an extra kettle of boiling water at hand in case the water level needs to be topped up after the filled jars are placed in the canner.

Place the lids, but not the screw bands, in hot water for 5 minutes immediately before using. This softens the sealing compound on the lids so that an airtight seal is formed. The screw bands should be at room temperature.

3. Filling Canning Jars

The processing time given in our recipes is based on the food being hot when it is put into the jars. It is important that the jars be processed immediately following the cooking stage. Remove each jar from canner as needed. A clean wide-mouth funnel is helpful to avoid spills when filling jars. Food may be ladled into the jar or poured using a small pitcher or measuring cup.

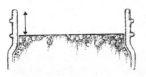

Leave proper headspace.

Leave a headspace to allow for expansion of food during processing. For most foods, a headspace of ½ inch (1 cm) is needed, although the headspace may be as little as ¼ inch (5 mm) for sweet spreads. If the jars are too full, the food may boil out and interfere with the formation of the seal. Too much headspace may result in the jar not sealing since the processing time is too short to drive out the extra air. We find it easiest to get in the habit of allowing ½ inch (1 cm) for all foods being processed.

Before placing a lid on the jar, be sure to remove air trapped between pieces of food. Any air bubbles can be released by sliding

courtesy of Bernardin

a clean small wooden or plastic spatula between the food and the jar and gently moving the food. The bubble should rise to the top. Failure to remove this trapped air can cause seal failure and may affect the color and storage quality of your preserved food. After releasing the trapped air, top up the liquid level if necessary by adding more food or liquid. Then wipe the rim and side of the jar with a clean cloth to remove any stickiness that could interfere with the formation of the vacuum seal.

Remove air bubbles

Remove a lid from the hot water and center it on the jar rim. Buy a magnetic lid lifter or glue a small magnet to the end of a wooden dowel rod to lift lids from the hot water. Then apply the screw band just until it is fingertip tight. Use only your fingertips! During processing, the air in the jar expands and is vented under the lid. When the jar cools, the air contracts and the lid "snaps" down, creating an airtight vacuum seal. If the lid is too tight, air cannot escape from the jar, possibly resulting in a failed seal.

4. Processing Canning Jars

Heating filled jars of food in boiling water for a specified time is called processing. Place the jars of filled food on the rack of a canner containing hot water. Adjust the water level to cover the jars by approximately

1 inch (2.5 cm). Cover the canner and bring water to a boil. Start counting the processing time called for in the recipe when the water has come to a steady boil. A kitchen timer is helpful for this. The water must remain at a full boil for the duration of the processing time. The processing time for each food is based on the size of the jar and the density and composition of the food, so follow times exactly. Under-processing can result in spoiled or off-flavored food and over-processing may overcook the food.

If you live at altitudes higher than 1,000 feet (305 m), longer processing times are needed. At higher altitudes water boils at a lower temperature. So it is necessary to increase processing time if you live at higher elevations. Adjust the time as follows:

- Elevations between 1,000 and 3,000 feet (305 and 915 m): add 5 minutes to the processing time given in the recipe.

- Elevations between 3,000 and 6,000 feet (915 and 1830 m): add 10 minutes to the processing time given in the recipe.

- Elevations between 6,000 and 8,000 feet (1,830 and 2,440 m): add 15 minutes to the processing time given in the recipe.

- Elevations between 8,000 and 10,000 feet (2,440 and 3,050 m): add 20 minutes to the processing time given in the recipe.

When the processing is finished, turn off the heat and remove lid from canner. Allow jars to remain in the water for 5 minutes to stabilize the pressure inside the jars. After 5 minutes remove the jars from the canner. Use a jar lifter or lift the rack from the water by its handles. Be sure not to tilt the jar to prevent the contents from running under the lid. Transfer the jars to a wooden cutting board or a surface covered with several layers of towels or newspaper. Do not place jars on a cold hard surface or they may break.

Do not dry jars or tighten the seal. Any water on top of jars will evaporate during the cooling period. Let the jars cool,

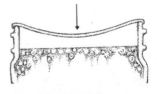

Cool jars for 12 to 24 hours;
check vacuum seal.
Sealed lids curve downwards.

undisturbed for 12 to 24 hours. Then check the seal. It is easy to tell if the jars are sealed as the metal lids curve downwards. (You can refrigerate any jars that are not sealed and use the contents for up to three weeks.) Remove the screw bands, dry them and store separately. If you prefer, replace them loosely on the jar. The bands are not necessary for storage because the firm seal achieved by the preserving process is strong enough to keep the jar airtight.

5. Storing Preserved Food

When the jars are cool and you have checked the seals, attach labels with contents and date. Preserved foods are best kept in a dark, cool place. Light may cause food to darken and a heat source, such as hot pipes, a furnace or stove, may hasten the loss of quality. A dark closet or a storage area in the basement is ideal.

If our recipes and canning procedures are followed carefully, there should be no problem with spoilage. However, before you open a jar of preserved food, it is a good idea to look closely for any sign of spoilage like a bulging lid or any leakage. The lid should be tight and give resistance when opened. If the lid is loose, or if the food has any off-flavors or mold on the surface, the food must be discarded. Don't take any chances. Plan to use preserved foods within a year. As long as the seal is secure, there is no risk of spoilage for a much longer time, but the quality of the food will deteriorate with extended storage.

EASY STEP-BY-STEP REMINDER
AS YOU WORK

- **20 Minutes Before Processing** (page 14)   Place jars in canner and add hot water. Cover canner and begin heating over medium heat. Keep jars hot until you are ready to fill them. If the recipe requires a preparation and cooking time longer than 20 minutes, begin preparation of the ingredients first. Then begin heating the water and jars in the canner while the prepared food is cooking. If the ingredients require a shorter preparation and cooking time, begin heating the canner before you start your recipe.

- **5 Minutes Before Processing** (page 14)   Place lids in hot water and keep lids hot until you are ready to use them. Do not heat screw bands.

- **Filling Canning Jars** (page 14)   Remove jars from canner and ladle food into hot jars to within ½ inch (1 cm) of top rim. Remove trapped air bubbles and readjust headspace to desired level by adding more hot food and/or liquid. Wipe rim and side of jars to ensure a good seal. Lift lid from hot water and center on jar. Apply screw band until fingertip tight.

- **Processing Canning Jars** (page 15)   Place jars in canner and adjust water level to cover jars by 1 inch (2.5 cm). Cover canner and place over high heat. Once a full boil is reached, begin counting the processing time specified in recipe (a full boil must be maintained for the entire time required). At end of processing time, turn heat off, remove canner lid and leave jars in canner for 5 minutes. Then lift jars out and place on heat-safe work surface. Do not touch seals or dry jars. Let cool for 12 to 24 hours. Check jar seals (sealed lids turn downwards) and remove screw bands.

- **Storing Preserved Food** (page 16)   Label jars with contents and date and store in a cool, dark place. Any jars that do not seal within 24 hours must be refrigerated or reprocessed immediately using new lids.

Possible Causes for Seal Failure or Spoiled Food

- Food was not processed in the canner for the correct time. It is important to start counting processing time just after the water in the canner returns to a boil.

- Processing time was not adjusted for altitude.

- New sealing lids were not used or were not softened in hot water.

- Screw bands were put on too tight or were re-tightened after processing.

- Too much or insufficient head space was left in the jar.

- The jar was cracked before, during or after processing. Cracking during processing could result from adding cold water to a canner of filled jars, placing hot jars on a cold surface or using jars not designed to withstand boiling-water temperatures.

- The quantity of ingredients called for in the recipe were not measured accurately.

- The vinegar was not of the standard 5% acetic acid. Always use vinegars of known acidity for canning purposes.

Sweet Spreads

USING the many different fruits available throughout the year, the variety and marvelous flavors of your homemade sweet spreads will greatly exceed those of even the best commercial jams and spreads. The following pages contain a selection of spreads that feature exciting fruit combinations not even considered by commercial jam makers. Try them to liven up your breakfast table. And a gift jar of a homemade jam or other sweet spread is always appreciated. Remember to include the recipe with it.

Name That Spread!

Jams, preserves, jellies, marmalades, conserves and fruit butters all share the same characteristic consistency, thanks to a gel formed by pectin. What makes them different from one another is the size or absence of fruit pieces, the method of cooking and the addition of other ingredients. Fruit curds are unique because they are the only spread in this category thickened by eggs.

Jam is a mixture of fruit and sugar made either from fruits that are high in pectin content or with added pectin. The fruit is usually chopped very finely or mashed.

A **preserve** is the same as a jam but the fruit is in larger pieces.

Jelly is the same as jam except that the cooked fruit has been strained to give a clear spread. Jellies are usually made from fruits high in pectin or with added pectin.

Marmalade is a jam made from citrus fruit. Marmalades generally do not have pectin added since citrus rinds and seeds contain enough pectin to form a soft gel.

A **conserve** is a jam with the addition of nuts, dried fruits and often spices.

Fruit butter is a sweet spread made by cooking fruit pulp with sugar until it has a thick, smooth consistency with no liquid remaining. Spices are often added.

Fruit curd is a sweet spread made from citrus fruit, sugar, butter and eggs cooked gently until thickened.

Four Essential Sweet Spread Ingredients

Four ingredients are essential for making sweet spreads: fruit, sugar, pectin and acid. But it isn't enough that these four substances are present—the proportion among them is critical to forming a gel. Following tested recipes, such as the ones found in this book or those supplied by pectin manufacturers, gives the best chance of success. To add flavor we like to suggest such extras as small amounts of liqueurs, nuts, spices and citrus zest. Generally, these are added at the last minute just before bottling.

1. Fruit

Fruit for all sweet spreads should be firm and ripe and always of good quality. Never use overripe fruit, since pectin disappears as fruit ripens, resulting in a jam that may not form a gel. Slightly underripe fresh fruit contains the most pectin, especially important for making spreads with no added pectin. Irregular-shaped fruit or fruit that is scarred is perfectly good, but discard any that is spoiled or moldy. Always wash or rinse fruit before use to remove any traces of dust, dirt or chemicals.

Fruit frozen without sugar, or with just a small amount of sugar, is great for making jam and other sweet spreads. Plan to freeze such fruits as rhubarb, berries and cherries when they are plentiful to make into jam later at your convenience. Choose clean, slightly underripe fruits at the peak of the growing season. Place the fruit in single layers on shallow cookie trays in the quantities required for each recipe you plan to use. Freeze the trays of fruit and then package in airtight labeled containers. The natural flavor is better preserved by adding a small amount of sugar (note the amount for the quantity of fruit so you can subtract it later from the sugar called for in the recipe). When you use the frozen fruit to make a sweet spread, there is no need to defrost it first. Just use it in the recipe as you would fresh fruit.

2. Sugar

Sugar is a vital ingredient in all sweet spreads. It links with the pectin to form a gel and high concentrations prevent the growth of micro-organisms. Sugar enhances the natural flavor of the fruit, so for that reason, a combination of a little sugar with an artificial sweetener is often used for our Light 'n' Low Sugar Spreads.

Timing the addition of sugar affects the texture of the fruit used in sweet spreads. If fruit and sugar are simply cooked together, the fruit quickly breaks down. However, when sugar is combined with fruit for several hours before cooking, the fruit shrinks as part of its juice is drawn out. This partially dehydrated fruit keeps its shape in the finished spread. Our Elegant Oven Strawberry Jam (page 28) is a perfect example of this process.

3. Pectin

Pectin is a naturally occurring gum-like substance found in many fruits and vegetables. Fruits contain pectin in varying amounts depending on ripeness, variety and growing conditions. Pectin concentration is greatest in the cores, seeds and skins of the fruit and decreases considerably as the fruit ripens. Pectin molecules link with sugar and acid to form the gel that gives sweet spreads their smooth, semi-solid consistency. Some fruits may have enough pectin to make spreads that set well, while others require added pectin.

Adding pectin to the fruit often produces a spread with a fresher taste, and it allows fully ripe fruit to be used. It also shortens cooking time since there is no need to concentrate the natural pectin before a gel can form. The set cooking time of added-pectin recipes means there is no question as to when the spread is done. Since more sugar is required when pectin is added to a recipe, the yield from a given amount of fruit increases. Three sources of pectin are available for making sweet spreads:

Commercial pectin: Commercial pectin is a concentrated extract from high-pectin fruits such as apples and citrus fruits. It is available in liquid and dry form, which are not interchangeable. We have used both in testing our recipes. Be sure to check the "best before" date on the package.

Homemade apple pectin: Make your own pectin extract from apples (page 46). This interesting source allows you to make a very small amount of jam with just a few pieces of fruit.

High-pectin/low-pectin fruits: Combine high-pectin fruits with low pectin-ones to provide the required level of pectin. Adding apple (high pectin) to rhubarb (low pectin) or red currants (high pectin) to raspberries (low pectin) are good examples.

Guide to Pectin Content of Fruits

High-Pectin Fruits	High-Pectin Fruits
apples (sour* and sweet)	apricots*
cherries (sour* and sweet)	blueberries
crabapples*	elderberries
cranberries*	figs
currants (red* and black*)	nectarines
gooseberries*	peaches
grapefruit*	pears
grapes*	pineapple
kiwifruit*	raspberries*
lemons,* limes*	rhubarb*
oranges*	strawberries*
plums (some kinds)*	
quinces	

Fruits marked with an asterisk (*) are high in the acid
needed to combine with pectin for gel formation.

4. Acid

As well as having adequate pectin, fruit must contain the correct amount of acid to form a gel. Too much acid will form a gel that sets too quickly and too firmly, making the sweet spread "weep" as moisture is squeezed out. Marmalades often have too much acid so baking soda is added to reduce their acidity. Too little acid prevents a gel from forming so lemon juice is added to low-acid fruits to increase their acidity.

Two Tests For Determining Gel Formation

The balance between fruit, sugar, pectin and acid is critical for gel formation. This balance is a delicate one, so it is essential to measure all ingredients accurately. Do not change the prescribed amounts, especially the amounts of sugar and acid. Always use tested recipes. Even then, a gel is not guaranteed, because the amounts of natural sugar, pectin and acid in the fruit vary due to weather and storage conditions. Some types of gels, especially in marmalades, may require several hours or even days for the pectin to set. Others form quickly, even before complete cooling. In general, marmalades and conserves form a lighter gel than jams and jellies. Do not make double recipes of sweet spreads as the longer cooking time required for a larger amount may cause the pectin to break down, preventing a gel from forming. There are two tests to determine when a sweet spread will form a gel.

1. Freezer Test

Place two or three small plates in the freezer ahead of time. Test for gel formation by putting a spoonful of hot fruit mixture on one chilled plate. Immediately return it to the freezer and wait for 2 minutes. Meanwhile, remove the saucepan from the heat source to prevent overcooking. If the mixture is sufficiently cooked, it will form a gel that moves slowly as the plate is tilted. If it runs off the plate, cook for another 2 minutes and repeat until freezer test indicates a gel is formed.

2. Sheet or Spoon Test

Begin cooking. Test for gel formation by periodically dipping a cool metal spoon into the hot fruit mixture and immediately lifting the spoon

Spoon Test

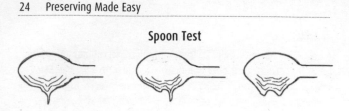

so the mixture runs off. At first the drops will be light and syrupy. As the mixture continues to cook, the drops from the spoon will become heavier. When the mixture "sheets" from the spoon (the drops become very thick and two drops run together before dropping off), it will form a gel on cooling and no further cooking is required.

Processing Sweet Spreads

Sweet spreads are processed by freezing or by processing in a boiling-water canner for 10 minutes. Detailed instructions for boiling-water processing are found on page 14. Note that canning jars with two-piece closures must be used to get an airtight seal when using the boiling-water procedure. Processing sweet spreads often allows the fruit to rise to the top. Stir before serving to break the gel and distribute the fruit. If not processed or frozen, sweet spreads may be stored in the refrigerator for up to 3 weeks.

For many years paraffin wax was used to seal jam jars, but it is no longer recommended. A layer of paraffin on top of a sweet spread does not give the necessary airtight seal. Molds may grow in the small cracks and pinholes that occur as the wax cools. We used to think that simply removing any mold appearing on the sweet spread was sufficient to make it safe. However, research has since found that mold growth may produce harmful substances that can penetrate unseen throughout the jar. So invest in some of the small canning jars that may be processed in a boiling-water bath. They are safe as well as attractive!

chapter 1

JAMS

GRACE your breakfast table with spreads few commercial jam-makers even think of. When you make your own, even the common ones are more concentrated and flavorful. You'll find nothing in a store to match our Peach Lavender Jam (page 45).

The wide variety of fruits available year-round make "in season" and "out of season" distinctions less important to home jam-makers. Even so, fresh, locally grown fruits at the peak of their growing season are still the most flavorful. But frequently we are simply too busy when local fruit is most plentiful to preserve all that we would like. So, use your freezer to store fruit until you are ready to use it. Measure, bag and label fruits by recipe, then freeze. Make your frozen treasures into fresh-tasting jams during the long winter months. And there is no problem with using previously frozen fruit in a freezer jam that will again be frozen for longer storage.

We have discovered that adding warmed sugar to our uncooked freezer jams helps the sugar to dissolve in the fruit. This process is also useful in Old-Fashioned Raspberry Jam (page 41), as raspberries are low in pectin. Warmed sugar dissolves faster in the simmering fruit, thereby protecting the pectin from breaking down.

Homemade Apple Pectin (page 48), made when apples are plentiful, can be used with any quantity of fruit. This allows you to make as little as one jar of jam. Thus, small quantities of leftover fruit can be readily converted into interesting jam. One day we had a couple of pears approaching ripeness. Adding a few frozen blueberries along with apple pectin, sugar and lemon juice made one jar of a great-tasting jam. With apple pectin handy on the shelf, preparing the jam took less than 20 minutes.

Some fruits you may want to use for jam do not contain enough pectin to form a gel in a reasonable cooking time. To get a nice gel in a short cooking time, add commercial pectin, our Homemade Apple Pectin (page 48) or fruits with a higher pectin content.

Serving Suggestions:

Add jam to some plain yogurt to make personalized fruit-flavored yogurts. Or mix yogurt, jam and a ripe banana in a blender to make a refreshing smoothie. Jams can be used to make a quick trifle. Spread ladyfingers with jam and top with a custard sauce. Spoonfuls of jam are a perfect topping for a plain cheesecake or a filling for a jelly roll cake. And, of course, breakfast toast would be nothing without jam.

A small amount of sugar added to fruit that is being frozen results in better flavor retention. But remember to reduce the sugar in your recipe by the amount added to the frozen fruit.

List of Recipes: Jams

Elegant Oven Strawberry Jam

An early version of this "amazingly successful" recipe appeared in
The Laura Secord Canadian Cookbook under the name of Sunshine
Strawberry Jam. The briefly cooked berries were set in the sun for 2 to
3 days to allow evaporation. Modern convection ovens greatly speed
up this process and avoid the problem of "crawlies" getting to the
jam before it is finished.

8 cups	halved or quartered firm strawberries,	
	(depending on size)	2 L
4 cups	granulated sugar	1 L
¼ cup	balsamic vinegar or lemon juice	50 mL

1. Combine berries and sugar in a very large stainless steel or enamel
   saucepan. Let stand for 2 hours, stirring several times.
2. Add vinegar and bring to a boil over high heat; reduce heat and
   boil gently, uncovered, for 10 minutes.
3. Pour into two 13 x 9-inch (3.5 L) glass baking dishes and place in
   a convection or standard oven at 150°F (65°C). Bake until mixture
   is thickened and will form a gel (see page 23), about 3 hours for
   convection and 10 hours for standard, stirring occasionally.
4. Ladle into hot jars and process for 10 minutes as directed on page
   14 (Easy Step-by-Step Preserving).

Makes 4 cups (1 L).

Variation:

Herb Strawberry Jam

Insert a sprig of fresh mint or basil in each jar before filling with jam.

Favorite Strawberry Jam

Generations have made strawberry jam to preserve this favorite summer fruit. Traditionally, low-pectin strawberries are cooked for long periods to achieve a gel. Our method uses standing periods alternating with much shorter cooking times. It makes a jam that retains its lovely red color and fresh flavor.

4 cups	halved or quartered firm strawberries, (depending on size)	1 L
2 cups	granulated sugar	500 mL
¼ cup	lemon juice	50 mL

1. Mix berries and sugar and let stand for 8 hours, stirring occasionally.
2. Place berry mixture in a medium stainless steel or enamel saucepan. Bring to a boil over medium heat. Add lemon juice, return to a boil and boil rapidly for 5 minutes. Remove from heat, cover and let stand for 24 hours.
3. Bring berries to a full boil over high heat and boil rapidly for 5 minutes, stirring constantly. Remove from heat.
4. Ladle into hot jars and process for 10 minutes as directed on page 14 (Easy Step-by-Step Preserving).

Makes 2½ cups (625 mL).

Variation:

Strawberry Rhubarb Jam
Add 1 cup (250 mL) finely chopped rhubarb to strawberries in step 1.

Makes 3 cups (750 mL).

Sherried Strawberry Preserve

Whole strawberries with a hint of sherry are suspended in this delight-ful preserve. A perfect accompaniment to fresh biscuits. Stir before serving to break gel and distribute fruit.

5 cups	whole small firm strawberries (about 2½ pints)	1.25 L
4 cups	granulated sugar	1 L
3 tbsp	lemon juice	45 mL
1	pouch liquid fruit pectin	1
½ cup	medium-dry sherry	125 mL

1. Stir together berries, sugar and lemon juice in a large bowl. Cover and let stand for 4 hours, stirring occasionally.
2. Place berries in a very large stainless steel or enamel saucepan. Bring to a boil over high heat and boil rapidly for 2 minutes, stir-ring constantly. Remove from heat; stir in pectin and sherry.
3. Ladle into hot jars and process for 10 minutes as directed on page 14 (Easy Step-by-Step Preserving).

Makes 5½ cups (1.4 L).

Variation:

Strawberry Preserves with White Wine
Use white wine in place of the sherry for a more delicate flavor.

Fresh Fig and Strawberry Jam

This jam is so good it disappears from the shelf. The fresh figs lend an amazing texture and taste to the strawberries. Be sure to make as much of it as jar and cupboard space allows whenever you can get your hands on fresh figs. Otherwise you may be like Margaret—she raved about it and then gave away so many jars she didn't have any left for herself!

1 lb	fresh green figs, stemmed and cut into small pieces	500 g
2 cups	quartered firm strawberries	500 mL
2 cups	granulated sugar	500 mL
3 tbsp	lemon juice	45 mL

1. Place figs, strawberries, sugar and lemon juice in a medium stainless steel or enamel saucepan. Cover and let stand for 1 hour, stirring occasionally.
2. Bring to a boil over high heat, reduce heat to medium and boil rapidly, uncovered, until mixture will form a gel (see page 23), about 15 minutes, stirring frequently. Remove from heat.
3. Ladle into hot jars and process for 10 minutes as directed on page 14 (Easy Step-by-Step Preserving).

Makes about 4 cups (1 L).

tip

Fresh figs have a longer season than we realized. California figs are ready in May and are also available from Greece and Italy in late summer and fall. If you missed them, occasionally you can find figs from South America in the late fall and early winter. Remember that fresh figs are extremely perishable and should be used as soon as possible after purchase. They may be stored in a refrigerator for up to 3 days.

Festive Cranstrawberry Jam

This jam's ruby-rich appearance is just right with festive Christmas food. It adds great color to your breakfast table and wonderful taste to toast and muffins all year round.

1	pkg (15 oz/425 g) frozen sliced strawberries in light syrup, thawed	1
2 cups	fresh or frozen cranberries	500 mL
1	large unpeeled orange, cut into large pieces	1
3 cups	granulated sugar	750 mL
1	pouch liquid fruit pectin	1
2 tbsp	orange liqueur or frozen orange juice concentrate	25 mL

1. Place strawberries in a very large stainless steel or enamel sauce-pan.
2. Coarsely chop cranberries and orange in a food processor. Remove and add to saucepan. Stir in sugar. Bring to a full boil over high heat and boil hard for 2 minutes, stirring constantly. Remove from heat and stir in pectin and liqueur.
3. Ladle into hot jars and process for 10 minutes as directed on page 14 (Easy Step-by-Step Preserving).

Makes 6 cups (1.5 L).

Serving Suggestion:

Cinnamon Tortilla Roll-ups
An interesting use for this jam as well as many others.
Warm a small flour tortilla in either the microwave oven or in a non-stick skillet. Mix 1 tbsp (15 mL) each of plain low-fat yogurt, low-fat ricotta cheese and 1 tsp (5 mL) Festive Cranstrawberry Jam. Spread mixture evenly over tortilla, add a dash of ground cinnamon or nutmeg, roll up and enjoy.

Four Fruit Red Jam

Use fresh or frozen fruit, but remember to measure frozen fruit before thawing and thaw before crushing.

2 cups	raspberries or loganberries, crushed	500 mL
2 cups	red currants, crushed	500 mL
2 cups	sliced strawberries, crushed	500 mL
1½ cups	chopped sour cherries	375 mL
4 cups	granulated sugar	1 L
¼ cup	lemon juice	50 mL

1. Place raspberries, currants, strawberries, cherries, sugar and lemon juice in a large stainless steel or enamel saucepan. Cover and let stand for 10 minutes.
2. Bring to a boil over high heat, stirring constantly. Boil rapidly, uncovered, until mixture will form a gel (see page 23), about 15 minutes, stirring frequently. Remove from heat.
3. Ladle into hot jars and process for 10 minutes as directed on page 14 (Easy Step-by-Step Preserving).

Makes about 5 cups (1.25 L).

Serving Suggestion:

Red Fruit Sauce
This one is excellent for pancakes, French toast or waffles.
Melt ½ cup (125 mL) Four Fruit Red Jam in a small saucepan over low heat. Stir 1 tsp (5 mL) cornstarch into ½ cup (125 mL) cherry juice and ¼ cup (50 mL) water. Whisk into melted jam, boil gently, uncovered, over low heat until slightly thickened. Stir in ½ tsp (2 mL) ground cinnamon, a small amount of grated lemon rind and ½ cup (125 mL) sour cherries.

Makes about 1¾ cups (425 mL).

Red and Black Currant Cassis Jam

The strong, rich taste of two kinds of currants reinforced by a currant-based liqueur makes this a jam for the true currant lover. Currants are very high in pectin, so don't over cook them. They thicken up considerably after cooking.

2½ cups	black currants, washed and stemmed	625 mL
2½ cups	red currants, washed and stemmed	625 mL
1 cup	water	250 mL
3 cups	granulated sugar	750 mL
2 tbsp	lemon juice	25 mL
3 tbsp	Cassis liqueur *(see Tip)*	45 mL

1. Place currants and water in a large stainless steel or enamel saucepan. Bring to a boil over high heat, cover, reduce heat and boil gently for 10 minutes, stirring occasionally.
2. Add sugar, lemon juice and liqueur. Bring to a full boil over high heat, stirring constantly. Boil rapidly uncovered until mixture will form a gel (see page 23), about 10 minutes. Remove from heat.
3. Ladle into hot jars and process for 10 minutes as directed on page 14 (Easy Step-by-Step Preserving).

Makes 5 cups (1.25 L).

tip | *Cassis liqueur can be replaced with black currant Italian soda syrup.*

Sour Cherry Gooseberry Jam

Tart sour cherries wonderfully complement the sweet gooseberries in this simple recipe.

2 cups	**chopped pitted sour cherries**	
	(about 4 cups/1 L whole fruit)	500 mL
2 cups	**chopped gooseberries**	
	(about 2½ cups/625 mL whole fruit)	500 mL
1 cup	**water**	250 mL
4 cups	**granulated sugar**	1 L

1. Combine cherries, gooseberries and water in a large stainless steel or enamel saucepan. Bring to a boil, reduce heat, cover and boil gently for 15 minutes.
2. Add sugar, return to a full boil and boil rapidly, uncovered, until mixture will form a gel (see page 23), about 15 minutes, stirring frequently. Remove from heat.
3. Ladle into hot jars and process for 10 minutes as directed on page 14 (Easy Step-by-Step Preserving).

Makes 4 cups (1 L).

Gooseberry Rhubarb Jam

This combination of two tart, old-fashioned country garden fruits gives us a jam with a wonderful flavor and glorious color. If you are making this jam with frozen fruit, chop and measure while fruit is still frozen.

2 cups	finely chopped rhubarb	500 mL
½ cup	water	125 mL
2 cups	gooseberries, stems removed and coarsely chopped	500 mL
2 tbsp	lemon juice	25 mL
5½ cups	granulated sugar	1.375 L
1	pouch liquid fruit pectin	1

1. Place rhubarb and water in a very large stainless steel or enamel saucepan. Bring to a boil over high heat, reduce heat, cover and boil gently for 3 minutes.
2. Stir gooseberries, lemon juice and sugar into rhubarb. Return to a full boil over high heat and boil hard for 1 minute, stirring constantly. Remove from heat and stir in pectin.
3. Ladle into hot jars and process for 10 minutes as directed on page 14 (Easy Step-by-Step Preserving).

Makes 5 cups (1.25 L).

Gingered Rhubarb Jam With Honey

In England it's traditional to combine ginger with rhubarb. In this jam, ginger adds a pungent spiciness while honey offsets rhubarb's strong tartness.

1	lemon	1
2 cups	chopped fresh or frozen rhubarb	500 mL
1	large tart apple, peeled, cored and finely chopped	1
½ cup	water	125 mL
1½ cups	granulated sugar	375 mL
1 cup	liquid honey	250 mL
1½ tbsp	finely chopped Candied Ginger or crystallized ginger	20 mL

1. Remove thin outer rind from lemon with vegetable peeler and cut into fine strips with scissors or sharp knife; or use a zester. Place lemon rind in a medium stainless steel or enamel saucepan. Squeeze juice from lemon and reserve 1 tbsp (15 mL).
2. Add rhubarb, apple and water to saucepan. Bring to a boil over high heat, cover, reduce heat and boil gently for 15 minutes or until fruit is tender.
3. Add sugar, honey, ginger and reserved lemon juice. Return to a boil and boil rapidly, uncovered, until mixture will form a gel (see page 23), about 8 minutes, stirring frequently. Remove from heat.
4. Ladle into hot jars and process for 10 minutes as directed on page 14 (Easy Step-by-Step Preserving).

Makes 3¼ cups (800 mL).

Bluebarb Jam

Only by using frozen fruit can we make this wonderful jam from fruits having different growing seasons.

3½ cups	chopped fresh or frozen rhubarb	875 mL
½ cup	water	125 mL
2¼ cups	coarsely chopped fresh or frozen blueberries	550 mL
1 tbsp	lemon juice	15 mL
1	box regular powdered fruit pectin	1
5½ cups	granulated sugar	1.375 L

1. Place rhubarb and water in a very large stainless steel or enamel saucepan. Bring to a boil over high heat, cover, reduce heat, and simmer for 5 minutes, stirring often.
2. Add blueberries, lemon juice and pectin; mix well. Bring to a boil over high heat, stirring constantly. Add sugar, return to a full boil and boil hard for 1 minute, stirring constantly. Remove from heat. Ladle into hot jars and process for 10 minutes as directed on page 14 (Easy Step-by-Step Preserving).

Makes 6 cups (1.5 L).

Spiced Blueberry Honey Jam

Honey adds its own delicate nuance to the more defined blueberry
and nutmeg flavors in this delightful jam. It can be made any time
with frozen blueberries.

2½ cups	fresh or frozen coarsely chopped blueberries	625 mL
2½ cups	granulated sugar	625 mL
1 cup	liquid honey	250 mL
1 tbsp	lemon juice	15 mL
½ tsp	ground nutmeg	2 mL
1	pouch liquid fruit pectin	1

Place blueberries, sugar, honey, lemon juice and nutmeg in a large
stainless steel or enamel saucepan. Bring to a full boil over high heat and
boil hard for 2 minutes, stirring constantly. Remove from heat and stir in
pectin. Ladle into hot jars and process for 10 minutes as directed on page
14 (Easy Step-by-Step Preserving).

Makes 4 cups (1 L).

tip | *Use a small grater to grate the seed of a nutmeg for
freshest flavor.*

Raspberry and Blueberry Jam

The flavors of the two berries and the citrus fruit combine beautifully in this interesting jam. Make this jam year round from either fresh or frozen berries.

3 cups	fresh or frozen unsweetened raspberries	750 mL
2 cups	fresh or frozen unsweetened blueberries	500 mL
1	large orange	1
6½ cups	granulated sugar	1.625 L
2 tbsp	lemon juice	25 mL
1	pouch liquid fruit pectin	1

1. Mash raspberries and blueberries in a very large stainless steel or enamel saucepan.
2. Remove thin outer rind from orange with vegetable peeler and cut into fine strips with scissors or sharp knife; or use a zester. Add to saucepan. Remove and discard remaining white rind. Finely chop orange in food processor with on/off motion to measure ½ cup (125 mL). Add orange pulp, sugar and lemon juice to saucepan.
3. Bring fruit to a full boil over high heat and boil hard for 1 minute, stirring constantly. Remove from heat and stir in pectin.
4. Ladle into hot jars and process for 10 minutes as directed on page 14 (Easy Step-by-Step Preserving).

Makes 7 cups (1.75 L).

Variations:
Raspberry Cranberry Jam
Replace blueberries with 2 cups (500 mL) fresh or frozen cranberries, finely chopped.

Old-Fashioned Raspberry Jam

The intense raspberry flavor of this jam makes it a long-time favorite.
Warming the sugar beforehand keeps the jam boiling evenly and
ensures success.

| 4 cups | granulated sugar | 1 L |
| 4 cups | raspberries | 1 L |

1. Place sugar in an ovenproof shallow pan and warm in a 250°F
   (120°C) oven for 15 minutes. (Warm sugar dissolves better).
2. Place berries in a large stainless steel or enamel saucepan. Bring
   to a full boil over high heat, mashing berries with a potato masher
   as they heat. Boil hard for 1 minute, stirring constantly.
3. Add warm sugar, return to a boil and boil until mixture will form a
   gel (see page 23), about 5 minutes.
4. Ladle into hot jars and process for 10 minutes as directed on page
   14 (Easy Step-by-Step Preserving).

Makes 4 cups (1 L).

tip

*To make a small boiling-water canner, tie several screw
bands together with string or use a small round cake rack
in the bottom of a large covered Dutch oven. Be sure the
pan is high enough for 2 inches (5 cm) of water to cover
the jars when they are sitting on the rack.*

Raspberry Jam with Chambord

This elegant jam is an ideal gift for a special friend. The unparalleled flavor of fresh raspberries is wonderfully complemented by raspberry liqueur.

3¾	cups crushed raspberries	
	(about 5 cups/1.25 L whole berries)	925 mL
4 cups	granulated sugar	1 L
3 tbsp	lemon juice	45 mL
1	pouch liquid fruit pectin	1
⅓ cup	Chambord, Framboise or Raspberry Liqueur	75 mL

1. Combine berries, sugar and lemon juice in a very large stainless steel or enamel saucepan. Let stand for 10 minutes.
2. Place pan over high heat, bring to a full boil and boil hard for 2 minutes, stirring constantly. Remove from heat; stir in pectin and liqueur. Ladle into hot jars and process for 10 minutes as directed on page 14 (Easy Step-by-Step Preserving).

Makes 6 cups (1.5 L).

Cranberry Pear Lemon Jam

Combine these three distinctly flavored fruits for a delicious breakfast
jam. Its tart tangy flavor also marries well with roasted poultry and pork.

4	large Bartlett pears, peeled, cored and diced	
	(about 4 cups/1 L)	4
3 cups	coarsely chopped fresh or frozen cranberries	750 mL
½ cup	water	125 mL
2 tsp	grated lemon rind	10 mL
2 tbsp	lemon juice	25 mL
1¾ cups	granulated sugar	425 mL

1. Combine pears, cranberries, water and lemon rind in a large
   stainless steel or enamel saucepan. Bring to a boil over high heat,
   cover, reduce heat and cook for 5 minutes, stirring frequently.
2. Gradually add lemon juice and sugar, stirring until sugar is
   dissolved. Boil rapidly, uncovered, until mixture will form a
   gel (see page 23), about 15 minutes, stirring frequently.
   Remove from heat.
3. Ladle into hot jars and process for 10 minutes as directed on
   page 14 (Easy Step-by-Step Preserving).

Makes 5 cups (1.25 L).

Peach Pear Jam with Lime

Two fall fruits combine to make one of our favorite jams. This started off as Ellie's peach recipe. One day, with not enough peaches to make the jam, she added some pears. Since these fruits are best in season for making this jam, this is a larger recipe than many others.

	rind of 1 lime	
2 cups	finely chopped peeled peaches	500 mL
2 cups	finely chopped peeled pears	500 mL
1	box regular powdered fruit pectin	1
5 cups	granulated sugar	1.25 L

1. Remove thin outer rind from lime with vegetable peeler and cut into fine strips with scissors or sharp knife; or use a zester. Place lime rind in a small microwavable container with ¼ cup (50 mL) water. Microwave on High (100%) for 1 minute. Drain and discard liquid; reserve rind.
2. Place peaches, pears, lime rind and pectin in a very large stainless steel or enamel saucepan. Bring to a boil over high heat, stirring constantly. Add sugar, return to a full boil and boil hard for 1 minute, stirring constantly. Remove from heat.
3. Ladle into hot jars and process for 10 minutes as directed on page 14 (Easy Step-by-Step Preserving).

Makes 7 cups (1.75 L).

Peach Lavender Jam

Many people do not think of cooking with lavender, an edible herb
that subtly accents the flavor of fresh fruits such as peaches, strawberries, raspberries, orange and lemon, but it adds a wonderful flavor to
this jam.

2 tbsp	dried lavender flowers (*see Tip*)	25 mL
½ cup	boiling water	125 mL
4 cups	finely chopped peaches	1 L
	(about 5-6 medium peaches)	
2 tbsp	lemon juice	25 mL
6 cups	granulated sugar	1.5 L
1	pouch liquid fruit pectin	1

1. Place lavender flowers in a small bowl. Pour boiling water over
   flowers and steep for 20 minutes. Strain and discard flowers.
2. Combine lavender liquid, peaches, lemon juice and sugar in a very
   large stainless steel or enamel saucepan. Bring to a full boil over
   high heat and boil hard for 2 minutes, stirring constantly. Remove
   from heat and stir in pectin.
3. Ladle into hot jars and process for 10 minutes as directed on
   page 14 (Easy Step-by-Step Preserving).

Makes 6 cups (1.5 L).

tip | *Look for organically grown lavender at herb fairs and herb
specialty growers. For an added touch, place a small sprig
on top of jam before sealing.*

Spiced Wine Peach Jam

The spices and wine do interesting flavorful things to ordinary peaches in this sophisticated jam.

½ cup	golden raisins	125 mL
⅓ cup	dry red wine or juice	75 mL
4 cups	finely chopped peaches	
	(about 5 to 6 medium peaches)	1 L
3 tbsp	lemon juice	45 mL
1	box regular powdered fruit pectin	1
5 cups	granulated sugar	1.25 L
1 tsp	ground cinnamon	5 mL
½ tsp	ground allspice	2 mL

1. Bring raisins and wine to a boil in a small saucepan, remove from heat, drain and discard liquid.
2. Combine raisins, peaches, lemon juice and pectin in a very large stainless steel or enamel saucepan. Bring to a boil over high heat, stirring constantly. Add sugar, return to a full boil and boil hard for 1 minute, stirring constantly. Remove from heat and stir in cinnamon and allspice.
3. Ladle into hot jars and process for 10 minutes as directed on page 14 (Easy Step-by-Step Preserving).

Makes about 6 cups (1.5 L).

Variation:
Spiced Wine Pear Jam
Replace peaches with 4 cups (1 L) finely chopped pears. Ground nutmeg is an excellent substitution for the cinnamon.

Fresh Apricot Jam

This very easy-to-make recipe produces a lovely fresh-tasting jam. It may be all that is needed to spur a neophyte's interest in jam-making.

3 cups	coarsely chopped unpeeled fresh apricots	
	(about 2 lb/1 kg, or 14 to 20 apricots)	750 mL
3½ cups	granulated sugar	875 mL
¼ cup	lemon juice	50 mL

1. Stir together apricots, sugar and lemon juice in a large bowl. Cover and let stand at room temperature for 12 hours, stirring occasionally.
2. Place apricot mixture in a medium stainless steel or enamel saucepan. Bring to a boil over high heat, stirring frequently. Reduce heat to medium and boil rapidly, uncovered, until mixture will form a gel (see page 23), about 25 minutes, stirring frequently. Remove from heat.
3. Ladle into hot jars and process for 10 minutes as directed on page 14 (Easy Step-by-Step Preserving).

Makes about 3½ cups (875 mL).

Serving Suggestion:
Crunchy Apricot Breakfast Yogurt
In a small bowl, combine 1 cup (250 mL) plain or vanilla low-fat yogurt. Stir in ½ cup (125 mL) Fresh Apricot Jam and 1 cup (250 mL) granola-type cereal just before serving.

Makes about 2 cups (500 mL).

Homemade Apple Pectin

The pectin content of apples decreases during storage, so remember
to make this pectin in the fall when apples are at their freshest. The
straining process is made easier if the apple mixture is first pressed
through a coarse sieve to remove most of the solids and then strained
through several layers of cheesecloth or a jelly bag for extra clarity.

7	tart apples (about 2 lb/1 kg)	7
4 cups	water	1 L
2 tbsp	lemon juice	25 mL

1. Cut apples into quarters (do not peel or core). Combine with water
   and lemon juice in a large stainless steel or enamel saucepan.
   Bring to a boil over high heat, cover, reduce heat and simmer for
   40 minutes, stirring occasionally.
2. Strain through a coarse sieve and discard solids. Then pour liquid
   through a jelly bag or several layers of cheesecloth.
3. Ladle into hot jars and process for 10 minutes as directed on page
   14 (Easy Step-by-Step Preserving).

Makes 4 cups (1 L).

tip | *Use your imagination to combine your favorite fruits with
an equal amount of Homemade Apple Pectin for your own
signature breakfast spread.*

Gooseberry jam

Plums

Tomatoes

Peppers

Marmalade

Pickles

Suggested Fruit Combinations for Making Jam Using Homemade Apple Pectin:

- ½ cup (125 mL) chopped kiwifruit and ½ cup (125 mL) chopped mango.
- ½ cup (125 mL) chopped pears and ½ cup (125 mL) chopped blueberries.
- ½ cup (125 mL) chopped fresh pineapple and ½ cup (125 mL) chopped papaya.
- ½ cup (125 mL) chopped blueberries and ½ cup (125 mL) chopped plums.
- 1 cup (250 mL) frozen raspberries, thawed and mashed, with 1 tsp (5 mL) chopped fresh mint stirred in after cooking.
- 1 cup (250 mL) chopped sweet cherries, with ½ tsp (2 mL) lemon juice.

1. For each 1 cup (250 mL) finely chopped fruit, add 1 cup (250 mL) Homemade Apple Pectin and ¾ cup (175 mL) granulated sugar.
2. Combine fruit, pectin and sugar in a stainless steel or enamel saucepan. Add 1 tsp (5 mL) lemon juice if fruit is low acid (see chart on page 23). Bring to a boil over high heat and boil rapidly, uncovered, until mixture will form a gel (see page 23), about 10 to 15 minutes, stirring frequently.
3. Ladle into jars, cover and store in refrigerator for up to 3 weeks. If desired, process for 10 minutes as directed on page 14 (Easy Step-by-Step Preserving).

Each recipe makes about 1¼ cups (300 mL) jam.

Autumn Fruit Jam

Plums, apples and pears are all in season at the same time. Together they make a jam that reflects the luscious essence of early fall fruits. The high pectin content of plums and apples compensates for the low pectin in pears to produce a well-set jam.

5	plums, sliced	5
2	medium apples, peeled, cored and chopped	2
2	medium pears, peeled, cored and chopped	2
1 cup	water	250 mL
2 tsp	grated lemon rind	10 mL
2 tbsp	lemon juice	25 mL
3 cups	granulated sugar	750 mL
½ tsp	each: ground cinnamon and ginger	2 mL

1. Combine plums, apples, pears, water, lemon rind and lemon juice in a large stainless steel or enamel saucepan. Bring to a boil over high heat, cover, reduce heat and cook for 10 minutes or until fruit is softened.
2. Add sugar to fruit and return to a boil, stirring constantly until sugar is dissolved. Boil rapidly, uncovered, until mixture will form a gel (see page 23), about 30 minutes, stirring occasionally. Stir in cinnamon and ginger.
3. Ladle into hot jars and process for 10 minutes as directed on page 14 (Easy Step-by-Step Preserving).

Makes 4 cups (1 L).

Variations:
Replace cinnamon and ginger with 1 tbsp (15 mL) vanilla extract added to cooked jam just before bottling.

Plum and Crabapple Jam

Crabapples are more commonly used in jellies than jams. Combined
with plums they impart a sweet-tart flavor and a gorgeous color to this
quite different jam. Do not overcook it. Since plums and crabapples
are naturally high in pectin, this jam thickens considerably after it's
cooked.

3 cups	quartered unpeeled crabapples	
	(about 4 cups/1 L whole fruit)	750 mL
1½ cups	water	375 mL
1	cinnamon stick about 4 inches(10 cm) long	1
4 cups	sliced blue or purple plums	
	(about 8 large or 16 small plums)	1 L
5 cups	granulated sugar	1.25 L
¾ cup	dry red or white wine or grape juice	175 mL

1. Place crabapples, water and cinnamon stick in a very large stainless steel or enamel saucepan. Bring to a boil over high heat,
   cover, reduce heat and boil gently for 10 minutes or until fruit is
   soft. Remove from heat and discard cinnamon stick. Press crabapples through a sieve; discard solids.
2. Return crabapple pulp to saucepan. Add plums, sugar and wine.
   Bring to a full boil and boil rapidly, uncovered, until mixture will
   form a gel (see page 23), about 20 minutes, stirring frequently.
   Remove from heat.
3. Ladle into hot jars and process for 10 minutes as directed on page
   14 (Easy Step-by-Step Preserving).

Makes 6 cups (1.5 L).

Plum Amaretto Jam

The almond flavor of the liqueur nicely complements the tartness of the plums in this rich purple jam. Plums are seldom used for jam, but after tasting this one you'll want to take a plum to breakfast more often.

3 cups	**chopped tart red or purple plums**	
	(about 8 to 10 plums)	750 mL
3 cups	**granulated sugar**	750 mL
¼ cup	**water**	50 mL
3 tbsp	**lemon juice**	45 mL
¼ cup	**Amaretto liqueur (see Tip)**	50 mL

1. Combine plums, sugar, water and lemon juice in a large stainless steel or enamel saucepan.
2. Bring to a boil over high heat, reduce heat to medium and boil rapidly until mixture will form a gel (see page 23), about 20 minutes, stirring frequently. Remove from heat and stir in liqueur.
3. Ladle into hot jars and process for 10 minutes as directed on page 14 (Easy Step-by-Step Preserving).

Makes 4 cups (1 L).

Amaretto liqueur can be replaced with 1 tbsp (15 mL) of almond extract.

Mango Plum Jam

A great small-batch jam to make any time you find nice ripe mangoes.
Plums give an interesting flavor twist to the exotic sweet-tart flavor of
mangoes.

1 cup	finely chopped plums (about 3 to 4 plums)	250 mL
½ cup	water	125 mL
1	mango, peeled and diced	1
½	box regular powdered fruit pectin (*see Tip*)	½
1 tbsp	lemon juice	15 mL
3 cups	granulated sugar	750 mL

1. Place plums and water in a large stainless steel or enamel saucepan. Bring to a boil over high heat, cover, reduce heat and simmer
   for 10 minutes, stirring frequently.
2. Stir mango, pectin and lemon juice into plums; mix well. Return
   to a boil over high heat, uncovered, stirring constantly. Add sugar,
   return to a full boil and boil hard for 1 minute, stirring constantly.
   Remove from heat.
3. Ladle into hot jars and process for 10 minutes as directed on page
   14 (Easy Step-by-Step Preserving).

Makes 4 cups (1 L).

tip | *The remaining pectin can be used to make Microwave
Winter Pear Amaretto Jam (page 60).*

Festive Kiwifruit Daiquiri Jam

This is a favorite of people who like jams that are less sweet.

1½ cups	finely chopped kiwifruit (about 5 kiwifruit)	375 mL
⅓ cup	lime juice (about 2 limes)	75 mL
¼ cup	water	50 mL
2 tbsp	dried cranberries or cherries, coarsely chopped	25 mL
3 cups	granulated sugar	750 mL
1	pouch liquid fruit pectin	1
¼ cup	dark rum	50 mL

Place kiwifruit, lime juice, water, cranberries and sugar in a large stainless steel or enamel saucepan. Bring to a full boil over high heat and boil hard for 2 minutes, stirring constantly. Remove from heat; stir in pectin and rum. Ladle into hot jars and process for 10 minutes as directed on page 14 (Easy Step-by-Step Preserving).

Makes 4 cups (1 L).

Winter Pear and Apricot Jam

Bosc and Anjou pears keep for long periods, making them available
for most of the winter. The tartness of dried apricots combines with
the sweetness of pears to make a great winter jam.

½ cup	finely chopped dried apricots	125 mL
1¾ cups	water	425 mL
2 cups	finely chopped cored, peeled winter pears (Bosc or Anjou)	500 mL
2 tsp	lemon juice	10 mL
1	box regular powdered fruit pectin	1
4½ cups	granulated sugar	1.125 L

1. Soak apricots in water for 4 hours or overnight.
2. Pour apricots and liquid into a very large stainless steel or enamel
   saucepan. Add pears, lemon juice and pectin. Bring to a full boil over
   high heat, stirring constantly. Add sugar, return to a full boil and boil
   hard for 1 minute, stirring constantly. Remove from heat. Ladle into
   hot jars and process for 10 minutes as directed on page 14 (Easy
   Step-by-Step Preserving). Note that this jam is slow to set.

Makes 6 cups (1.5 L).

Australian Spiced Dried Fig Jam

Fig lovers will enjoy this succulent spread that Ellie discovered while in Australia. It is delicious as a cake and cookie filling.

8 oz	dried figs *(see Tip)*	250 g
2¼ cups	water	550 mL
4½ cups	granulated sugar	1.125 L
¼ tsp	ground cinnamon	1 mL
¼ tsp	ground nutmeg	1 mL
1	box regular powdered fruit pectin	1
1 tsp	grated lemon rind	5 mL
¼ cup	lemon juice	50 mL

1. Combine figs and water in a medium bowl. Let stand for 8 hours or overnight.
2. Drain figs, reserving liquid. Remove and discard stems and chop fruit finely. Place chopped fruit in a 4-cup (1 L) liquid measure and add reserved liquid and enough water to bring level to 3 cups (750 mL).
3. Combine sugar, cinnamon and nutmeg in a bowl. Set aside.
4. Place fig mixture, pectin, lemon rind and juice in a large stainless steel or enamel saucepan. Bring to a boil over high heat, stirring constantly. Add sugar-spice mixture, return to a full boil and boil hard for 1 minute, stirring constantly. Remove from heat.
5. Ladle into hot jars and process for 10 minutes as directed on page 14 (Easy Step-by-Step Preserving).

Makes 5 cups (1.25 L).

tip | *Since figs come in a variety of package sizes it is important to check the weight.*

Microwave Strawberry Lime Jam

You'll want to make a jar of this easy small-batch recipe when imported berries are available and you long for the taste of fresh strawberry
jam. The same goes for peaches.

1½ cups	granulated sugar	375 mL
2 cups	sliced, hulled strawberries	500 mL
2 tbsp	lime juice	25 mL

1. Place sugar and strawberries in two alternating layers in a deep
   12-cup (3 L) microwavable bowl. Pour lime juice over top. Do not stir.
2. Microwave, uncovered, on High (100%) for 5 minutes, stirring
   twice. Microwave, uncovered, on High for 10 minutes or until
   mixture will form a gel (see page 23), stirring every 4 minutes.
3. Ladle into hot jars and process for 10 minutes as directed on page
   14 (Easy Step-by-Step Preserving).

Makes 1½ cups (375 mL).

Variations:
Strawberry Lemon Jam: Replace lime juice with lemon juice.

Spiced Strawberry Jam: Tie 1 cinnamon stick, 2 whole cloves and
2 allspice berries loosely in cheesecloth and add to fruit during last
10 minutes of cooking. Remove and discard spice bag before bottling.

Peach Lime Jam: Prepare with same amount of peaches, sugar and
1 tbsp (15 mL) lime juice.

Microwave Ginger Plum Jam

Microwave purple plums anytime they are available for this small-batch, ginger–spiked jam. It takes about half an hour to prepare. Make a wonderful plum glaze for oven-roasted salmon by melting some of the jam and brushing it on the salmon while it is roasting.

3 cups	chopped purple plums (about 10 to 12 plums)	750 mL
2 cups	granulated sugar	500 mL
4 tsp	lemon juice	20 mL
¼ cup	finely chopped Candied Ginger	
	or crystallized ginger	50 mL

1. Place plums and sugar in a deep 8-cup (2 L) microwavable container. Stir in lemon juice.
2. Microwave, uncovered, on High (100%) for 7 minutes, stirring twice. Add ginger; microwave, uncovered, on High for 15 to 18 minutes or until mixture will form a gel (see page 23), stirring every 4 minutes.
3. Ladle into hot jars and process for 10 minutes as directed on page 14 (Easy Step-by-Step Preserving).

Makes 2½ cups (625 mL).

tip

Each summer, plums arrive in our markets in great variety—bright yellow and green (best known as greengage), iridescent red and dark purple. One fresh plum contains about 35 calories, which compares with 81 calories in a fresh apple and 100 in a fresh pear or banana. Plums are a very good low-calorie snack.

Microwave Peach Jam with Orange Liqueur

Intense peach flavor is highlighted by orange in this elegant and attractive jam.

3 cups	chopped fresh or frozen peaches	750 mL
2 cups	granulated sugar	500 mL
2 tbsp	lemon juice	25 mL
2 tbsp	orange liqueur or frozen orange juice concentrate, thawed	25 mL

1. Place peaches and sugar in a deep 8-cup (2 L) microwavable container. Stir in lemon juice.
2. Microwave, uncovered, on High (100%) for 7 minutes, stirring twice. Microwave, uncovered, on High for 12 to 15 minutes or until mixture will form a gel (see page 23), stirring every 4 minutes. Stir in liqueur.
3. Ladle into hot jars and process for 10 minutes as directed on page 14 (Easy Step-by-Step Preserving).

Makes 2 cups (500 mL).

tip | *If peaches are still frozen, you may need to add 2 to 3 minutes to the total cooking time.*

Microwave Winter Pear Amaretto Jam

The pear varieties found in winter, such as Bosc and Anjou, need the moist heat of microwave cooking to transform the relatively dry pears into a delicious jam. The almond of the liqueur highlights the taste of pears.

1½ cups	diced peeled winter pears (Bosc, Anjou)	375 mL
½ cup	chopped peeled tart apple	125 mL
2 tbsp	apple juice, cider or water	25 mL
½	box regular powdered fruit pectin (*see Tip*)	½
2 cups	granulated sugar	500 mL
1 tbsp	Amaretto liqueur	15 mL

1. Combine pears, apple, apple juice and pectin in a 3-quart (3 L) microwavable container. Microwave, uncovered, on High (100%) for 6 minutes or until mixture comes to a boil, stirring twice.
2. Add sugar. Microwave, uncovered, on High for 4 minutes or until mixture returns to a full boil and boil hard for 1 minute. Stir in liqueur.
3. Ladle into hot jars and process for 10 minutes as directed on page 14 (Easy Step-by-Step Preserving).

Makes 3 cups (750 mL).

tip | *The remaining half box of regular powdered fruit pectin can be used to make Mango Plum Jam (page 53).*

chapter 2

JELLIES

ONE of the best things about making jellies is their easy preparation—no peeling or coring, just wash, chop and use the lot. Jellies can be made from a variety of fruits and vegetables—berries, pears, apples, crabapples, plums, citrus fruits and sweet and hot peppers. Some of the very tastiest are made with wine and herbs.

Traditionally, jellies are made with the juice from cooked fruit strained through a clean jelly bag. A jelly bag is made of fabric with a sufficiently close weave to remove enough fruit pulp to ensure a clear jelly. You can buy one or you can line a colander or strainer with several layers of cheesecloth or an unused all-purpose cloth. Set the colander over a large bowl, pour in the fruit mixture and allow it to stand until the juice has drained through. This process can require up to several hours, but if you first press the fruit pulp through a coarse sieve to remove the larger solids, the resulting liquid will flow through the cloth much more quickly. The secret to a clear jelly is to let the juice drain through the cloth on its own. Avoid the temptation to squeeze out that last little bit of juice! Add sugar to the strained juice and cook until a gel stage is reached (see page 23). A properly set jelly retains its shape and quivers when removed from the jar.

Many of our recipes make jelly making even easier. They use prepared juices so there is no need for washing, chopping or straining. Peach Amaretto Jelly with Almonds (page 74) uses frozen peach nectar. Apple Cider Cinnamon Jelly (page 68) starts with fresh apple cider. Some herb and wine jellies fall into this "super-simple, quick and easy" category. A few jellies have some suspended fruit or vegetable pieces left in for eye-appeal and flavor. Commercial pectin, or our Homemade Apple Pectin (page 48), must be added to jellies made from juices that have not been cooked with their skins or seeds and to jellies made from fruits containing very little pectin.

Many flavorings can be added to jellies. Scented geranium leaves as well as herbs like lemon, thyme, mint and angelica give exciting interest to herb jellies. Examples of this treatment are our Sherried Rosemary Grape Juice Jelly (page 65) and Basic Herb Wine Jelly (page 67). Rose petals and even fruit leaves such as peach and plum impart an almond flavor. Try adding whole herbs of your choice to wine jellies.

Serving Suggestions:

Jellies have so many uses. We love the pepper jellies as appetizers with cream cheese and crackers. Our Cranberry Hot Pepper Jelly (page 70) and our wine jellies go superbly with chicken, turkey and duck. Roasted or broiled meats whether hot or cold, are greatly enhanced by Spiced Apple Jelly (page 69) and Apple Cranberry Wine Jelly (page 65). Of course, sweet jellies such as Tangerine Lemon (page 76), Grapefruit Raspberry Honey (page 71), and Red Currant and Raspberry Jelly (page 75) go wonderfully on rolls, hot biscuits and muffins. We are sure you will find your own favorite uses.

tip | *Give a jar of sparkling jelly as a hostess gift. Wrap it in a square of cellophane tied just above the lid and include the recipe.*

List of Recipes: Jellies

Wine Jellies

Wine jelly adds a wonderful flavor note to many meals. This basic recipe can be used with sherry, port, claret or Bordeaux. For a more delicate jelly, use white wine.

Basic Wine Jelly

2 cups	wine	500 mL
¼ cup	strained lemon juice	50 mL
3½ cups	granulated sugar	875 mL
1	pouch liquid fruit pectin	1

1. Place wine, lemon juice and sugar in a large stainless steel or enamel saucepan.Bring to a boil over high heat and boil hard for 1 minute, stirring constantly. Remove from heat and stir in pectin.
2. Ladle into hot jars and process for 10 minutes as directed on page 14 (Easy Step-by-Step Preserving).

Makes 4½ cups (1.125 L).

Cranberry Port Wine Jelly

Be sure to use pure cranberry juice. Beverages labeled "Beverage," "Drink" or "Cocktail" have been diluted and have a less-intense flavor.

1 cup	port or claret	250 mL
1 cup	pure cranberry juice	250 mL
3½ cups	granulated sugar	875 mL
1	pouch liquid fruit pectin	1

Proceed as for Basic Wine Jelly, substituting the cranberry juice for half of the wine.

Makes 4½ cups (1.125 L).

Sherried Rosemary Grape Juice Jelly

This delicate jelly has an affinity with poultry. The rosemary flavor also lends itself to pork or a leg of lamb.

1 cup	dry sherry	250 mL
1 cup	white grape juice	250 mL
3½ cups	granulated sugar	875 mL
1	pouch liquid fruit pectin	1
1	stem fresh rosemary, thyme or other fresh herb	1

Proceed as for Basic Wine Jelly, substituting grape juice for half of the wine. Add herb to each jar before processing.

Makes 4½ cups (1.125 L).

Apple Cranberry Wine Jelly

This special variation of traditional cranberry jelly is quickly prepared.

2½ cups	fresh or frozen cranberries	625 mL
4	large cooking apples, peeled, cored and chopped	4
1 cup	dry white wine	250 mL
1½ cups	granulated sugar	375 mL

1. Combine cranberries, apples and wine in a large stainless steel or enamel saucepan. Bring to a boil over high heat, cover, reduce heat and cook gently for 15 minutes or until fruit is soft. Strain through a sieve, discard pulp and return sieved liquid to saucepan.
2. Add sugar and return to a boil. Boil uncovered, until mixture forms a gel (see page 23), approximately 10 minutes, stirring frequently. Remove from heat.
3. Ladle into hot jars and process for 10 minutes as directed on page 14 (Easy Step-by-Step Preserving).

Makes 3 cups (750 mL).

Jellies Á l'herbe

Herbs give unique twists to jellies that make wonderful gifts. Making them is much like making tea: the herbs are steeped in boiling water or wine.

Basic Herb Jelly

Beautifully simple and sparkling jelly—serve with poultry, cheese and crackers, a cold meat salad plate or sliced meat sandwiches.

1¼ cups	water	300 mL
2 tbsp	chopped chopped fresh herb leaves or 2 tsp (10 mL) dried	25 mL
3½ cups	granulated sugar	875 mL
1 cup	juice	250 mL
2 tbsp	vinegar or lemon juice	25 mL
1	pouch liquid fruit pectin	1

1. Combine water and herb leaves in a small saucepan. Bring mixture to a boil; remove from heat. Cover and allow to steep for 5 minutes. Strain through a lined sieve; discard leaves.
2. Place 1 cup (250 mL) of the liquid in a large stainless steel or enamel saucepan; add sugar, juice and vinegar or lemon juice. Bring to a full boil over high heat and boil hard for 1 minute, stirring constantly. Remove from heat and stir in pectin.
3. Ladle into hot jars and process for 10 minutes as directed on page 14 (Easy Step-by-Step Preserving).

Makes about 4½ cups (1.125 L).

Basic Herb Wine Jelly

Use white wine if the jelly is to accompany poultry or pork, or red wine if it is to accompany red meats. Either way, it's a sparkling clear jelly enhanced with the flavor of your favorite herb. Some herbs to try are sage, basil, mint, savory, thyme, marjoram and oregano. The amount used may be increased or decreased according to individual taste preferences.

1¾ cups	dry white or red wine	425 mL
¼ cup	white or red wine vinegar	50 mL
3 tbsp	chopped fresh herb leaves or 1 tbsp (15 mL) dried	45 mL
3½ cups	granulated sugar	875 mL
1	pouch liquid fruit pectin	1

1. Combine wine, vinegar and herb leaves in a large stainless steel or enamel saucepan. Bring mixture to a boil; remove from heat. Cover and allow to steep for 30 minutes to extract flavors.
2. Strain mixture through a lined sieve; discard leaves. Return liquid to saucepan and stir in sugar. Bring to a boil over high heat and boil rapidly for 1 minute, stirring constantly. Remove from heat and stir in pectin.
3. Ladle into hot jars and process for 10 minutes as directed on page 14 (Easy Step-by-Step Preserving).

Makes 4 cups (1 L).

tip | *Add several garlic cloves to Basic Herb Wine Jelly made with white wine and rosemary for a perfect jelly to serve with a crown roast of lamb or lamb chops.*

Apple Cider Cinnamon Jelly

The full-bodied taste of fresh apple cider spiced with cinnamon is marvelous on toast and hot biscuits. Try heating the jelly and serve over pancakes or French toast. Reserve the cinnamon stick and add a small piece to each jar for an attractive garnish and more intense cinnamon flavor.

2½ cups	fresh-pressed apple cider	625 mL
1	stick cinnamon, 4 inches (10 cm),	
	broken into 4 pieces	1
3½ cups	granulated sugar	875 mL
1	pouch liquid fruit pectin	1

1. Combine cider and cinnamon pieces in a large stainless steel or enamel saucepan. Cover and bring to a boil over high heat, reduce heat and boil gently for 5 minutes. Strain cider through several layers of cheesecloth, reserving cinnamon pieces to add to jars. Rinse saucepan.
2. Measure 2 cups (500 mL) cider and return to saucepan; add sugar. Bring to a full boil over high heat, stirring constantly. Stir in pectin, return to a full boil and boil hard for 1 minute, stirring constantly. Remove from heat.
3. Ladle into hot jars, add one piece of cinnamon to each jar and process for 10 minutes as directed page 14 (Easy Step-by-Step Preserving).

Makes 4 cups (1 L).

Spiced Apple Jelly

We adapted this recipe from one Margaret's neighbor makes every fall using her own apples. Don't peel, core or remove the seeds and stems before cooking; they add pectin as well as color and flavor to the jelly. The crabapple variation is wonderful with poultry.

2 lb	apples, cut into large pieces (about 8 cups/2 L)	1 kg
6 cups	water	1.5 L
¼ cup	cider vinegar	50 mL
½ tsp	whole cloves	2 mL
2	cinnamon sticks, 3 inches (7.5 cm) long	2
1½ cups	granulated sugar	375 mL

1. Combine apples, water, vinegar, cloves and cinnamon sticks in a large stainless steel or enamel saucepan. Cover and bring to a boil over high heat, reduce heat and boil gently for 30 minutes. Strain mixture through a coarse sieve; discard solids. Pour liquid through a jelly bag.
2. Return strained liquid to pan and add sugar. Bring to a boil and boil rapidly, uncovered, until mixture will form a gel, (see page 23) about 15 minutes, stirring occasionally. Remove from heat.
3. Ladle into hot jars and process for 10 minutes as directed on page 14 (Easy Step-by-Step Preserving).

Makes 2 cups (500 mL).

Variation:
Spiced Crabapple Jelly
Replace apples with the same weight of crabapples.

Cranberry Hot Pepper Jelly

The color is as intense as the flavor of this sparkling red jelly. Adding cranberry to popular pepper jelly makes it perfect for the festive season. Keep it on hand for an easy appetizer with cream cheese on crackers, or to accompany any roast meat, especially game such as venison. Our version has medium heat, but you may easily change it by adding or omitting a jalapeño pepper.

1	large sweet red pepper	1
2	jalapeño peppers, seeded, or other hot pepper	2
¼ cup	water	50 mL
¾ cup	cider vinegar	175 mL
¾ cup	frozen cranberry cocktail concentrate, thawed	175 mL
3 cups	granulated sugar	750 mL
1	pouch liquid fruit pectin	1

1. Finely chop sweet and jalapeño peppers in food processor. Place in a small saucepan with water and vinegar. Bring mixture to a boil, cover, reduce heat and boil gently for 10 minutes. Strain mixture through a coarse sieve, pressing with back of a spoon to extract as much liquid as possible; discard solids. Pour liquid through a jelly bag.
2. Place strained liquid, cranberry concentrate and sugar in a medium stainless steel or enamel saucepan. Bring to a full boil over high heat, stirring constantly. Stir in pectin, return to a full boil and boil hard for 1 minute, stirring constantly. Remove from heat.
3. Ladle into hot jars and process for 10 minutes as directed on page 14 (Easy Step-by-Step Preserving).

Makes 3 cups (750 mL).

Grapefruit Raspberry Honey Jelly

With the bright color of raspberry and hint of honey, this jelly will become an instant favorite.

2	grapefruit, coarsely chopped	2
3 cups	water	750 mL
3 cups	fresh or frozen unsweetened raspberries	750 mL
3 cups	granulated sugar	750 mL
1 cup	liquid honey	250 mL

1. Place grapefruit and water in a medium stainless steel or enamel saucepan. Bring to a boil over high heat, cover, reduce heat and boil gently for 20 minutes. Add raspberries, return to a boil and boil gently for 5 minutes.
2. Pour fruit through a coarse strainer, pressing pulp to extract juice. Discard solids. Pour liquid through a jelly bag.
3. Return strained liquid to pan and add sugar and honey. Bring to a boil and boil rapidly, uncovered, until mixture will form a gel (see page 23), about 15 minutes, stirring occasionally. Remove from heat.
4. Ladle into hot jars and process for 10 minutes as directed on page 14 (Easy Step-by-Step Preserving).

Makes 2 cups (500 mL).

Jalapeño Mint Jelly

Jalapeño peppers and a double hit of mint liven up traditional mint jelly. Try it with crackers and cheese and with lamb or chicken.

1¾ cups	finely chopped fresh mint, divided	425 mL
1½ cups	water	375 mL
3½ cups	granulated sugar	875 mL
¾ cup	cider vinegar	175 mL
2 tbsp	strained fresh lemon juice	25 mL
2	jalapeño peppers, finely chopped	2
1	pouch liquid fruit pectin	1

1. Bring 1½ cups (375 mL) mint and water to a boil in a small saucepan. Remove from heat, cover and let stand for 30 minutes to steep. Strain through a lined sieve pressing with the back of a spoon to extract as much liquid as possible; discard mint.
2. Combine mint liquid, sugar, vinegar, lemon juice and peppers in a large stainless steel or enamel saucepan. Bring to a full boil over high heat and boil hard for 2 minutes, stirring constantly. Remove from heat; stir in pectin and remaining mint.
3. Ladle into hot jars and process for 10 minutes as directed on page 14 (Easy Step-by-Step Preserving).

Makes 4 cups (1 L).

Variation:
Lemon Balm Jelly
Use lemon balm leaves in place of the mint and omit the jalapeño peppers.

Sparkling Sweet Pepper Jelly

Pieces of red, yellow and orange pepper sparkle like jewels in this exotic jelly. Our favorite way to serve it is with cream cheese spread on melba toast rounds. We also like it with a sliver of Cheddar cheese on a cracker. If you like your pepper jelly hot, see the variation below.

½ cup	each: evenly diced sweet red, orange and yellow pepper	125 mL
¾ cup	white wine vinegar	175 mL
3 cups	granulated sugar	750 mL
1	pouch liquid fruit pectin	1

1. Combine peppers, vinegar and sugar in a medium stainless steel or enamel saucepan. Bring to a full boil over high heat and boil hard for 1 minute, stirring constantly. Add pectin; return to a boil and boil rapidly for 1 minute. Remove from heat.
2. Ladle into hot jars and process for 10 minutes as directed on page 14 (Easy Step-by-Step Preserving).

Makes 3½ cups (875 mL).

Variations:
Sparkling Hot Pepper Jelly
Use 2 jalapeño peppers, seeded and diced, to replace the yellow or orange pepper.

Sparkling Apricot Hot Pepper Jelly
Use 2 jalapeño peppers, seeded and diced, to replace the yellow pepper and use ¼ cup (50 mL) chopped dried apricots, soaked in water for 4 to 6 hours, to replace the orange pepper.

Peach Amaretto Jelly with Almonds

While in Arizona, Margaret found a beautiful sparkling peach jelly with floating slices of almonds. This is her version.

2 cups	strained peach nectar	500 mL
¼ cup	strained lemon juice	50 mL
3½ cups	granulated sugar	875 mL
1	pouch liquid fruit pectin	1
2 tbsp	amaretto liqueur	25 mL
¼ cup	sliced almonds	50 mL

1. Combine nectar, lemon juice and sugar in a large stainless steel or enamel saucepan. Bring to a full boil over high heat and boil hard for 1 minute, stirring constantly. Remove from heat and stir in pectin and liqueur.
2. Ladle into hot jars. Divide almonds between jars and stir into jelly. Process for 10 minutes as directed on page 14 (Easy Step-by-Step Preserving).

Makes 4 cups (1 L).

tip

During processing, you will find that the almonds have floated to the top of the jelly. Stir them into the jelly to redistribute them after opening.

Frozen concentrated peach cocktail, which comes in 12-oz/341 mL cans, may be prepared using 2 parts water rather than 3. Use it to replace peach nectar, reducing sugar to 3 cups (750 mL) because the peach cocktail already contains sugar.

Red Currant and Raspberry Jelly

The high pectin content of red currants makes them a perfect partner for raspberries, which have much less pectin. The resulting intense red jelly has an exquisite flavor for serving on hot biscuits or muffins. When melted, it makes a wonderful red-hued glaze for a simple fresh fruit tart.

2 cups	red currants, stemmed	500 mL
¾ cup	water	175 mL
2 cups	raspberries	500 mL
1⅓ cups	granulated sugar	325 mL

1. Using a potato masher, crush currants in a very large stainless steel or enamel saucepan. Add water and bring to a boil over high heat, reduce heat, cover and boil gently for 10 minutes. Add raspberries, return to a boil and boil gently for 3 minutes.
2. Strain mixture through a coarse sieve, pressing pulp to extract juice; discard solids. Pour juice through a jelly bag.
3. Return juice to saucepan, add sugar and bring to a full boil. Boil rapidly, uncovered, until mixture will form a gel (see page 23), about 10 minutes, stirring frequently.
4. Ladle into hot jars and process for 10 minutes as directed on page 14 (Easy Step-by-Step Preserving).

Makes 1¾ cups (425 mL).

Tangerine Lemon Jelly

We love this jewel-like jelly on hot biscuits or with cream cheese and bagels. For a special gift, add a sprig of fresh rosemary to the jelly before processing.

3	lemons	3
9–10	tangerines	9–10
1	box regular powdered fruit pectin	1
4½ cups	granulated sugar	1.125 L

1. Squeeze lemons and tangerines to give 4 cups (1 L) juice. Bring juice to a boil over high heat in a large stainless steel or enamel saucepan, cover, reduce heat and simmer for 10 minutes, stirring occasionally. Remove from heat.
2. Strain juice through a jelly bag. Return strained liquid to saucepan and stir in pectin. Bring to a full boil over high heat, reduce heat and boil gently for 1 minute, stirring constantly. Add sugar, return to a full boil and boil hard for 1 minute, stirring constantly. Remove from heat.
3. Ladle into hot jars and process for 10 minutes as directed on page 14 (Easy Step-by-Step Preserving).

Makes 5½ cups (1.375 L).

tip | *To obtain a very clear jelly without a jelly bag, strain the liquid through a lined sieve. We have found disposable cloth works really well for this.*

Tropical Fruit Jelly

It's our great fortune to have access to the wonderful exotic flavors of tropical fruits. Passion fruit, mango and papaya combine to give this jelly a truly tropical flavor. Passion fruit juice is worth the effort to find. Look in specialty shops selling Indian and Pacific Rim foods. Be sure to buy the one with no added water.

1½ cups	passion fruit juice	375 mL
½	mango, peeled and cubed	½
½	papaya, peeled, seeded and cubed	½
½ cup	water	125 mL
¼ cup	lime juice	50 mL
1 tsp	grated lime rind	5 mL
3½ cups	granulated sugar	875 mL
1	pouch liquid fruit pectin	1

1. Combine passion fruit juice, mango, papaya and water in a large stainless steel or enamel saucepan. Bring to a boil over high heat, reduce heat, cover and boil gently for 15 minutes. Add lime juice and rind. Remove from heat.
2. Strain juice through a coarse sieve, pressing pulp to extract as much liquid as possible; discard solids. Pour juice through a jelly bag (there should be 2 cups/500 mL—if not, top up with extra passion fruit juice).
3. Combine strained liquid and sugar in saucepan. Bring to a full boil over high heat, stirring constantly. Stir in pectin, return to a full boil and boil hard for 1 minute, stirring constantly. Remove from heat.
4. Ladle into hot jars and process for 10 minutes as directed on page 14 (Easy Step-by-Step Preserving).

Makes 4 cups (1 L).

chapter 3

MARMALADES

MARMALADES, similar to jams, always include the pulp of one or more citrus fruits—oranges, lemons, grapefruits, limes and tangerines. The citrus rind is suspended in the mixture to intensify the citrus flavor and to add color and texture. Other fruits are sometimes added to create mouth-watering combinations—for example, try our Blueberry Orange Marmalade or our Pear Apple Ginger Marmalade (pages 82 and 92).

Since citrus fruits are high in pectin, most cooked marmalades require no added pectin to set. The white portion of the rind and the seeds, which are used in many marmalade recipes, is where most of the pectin is found. The rind and seeds are discarded after cooking if their bitter flavor is not wanted in the finished marmalade. Since only the thin outer rind of the citrus fruit is used, it does not contain sufficient pectin to make the gel.

The very best time to make marmalade is during the winter when citrus fruits are at their best quality and lowest price. The bitter Seville-type oranges are available only for a short time during late January and early February. However, you can prolong this short season by freezing the oranges whole and then making our superb Traditional English Seville Marmalade (page 81) when time permits.

Marmalades do take a bit of time, but are well worth the effort. Citrus zesters, vegetable peelers, juice extractors and food processors take much of the labor out of their preparation.

Not all marmalades are bittersweet, as many people think. They range from a sweet Microwave Gingered Peach Marmalade (page 95) to an Old-Fashioned Tomato Marmalade (page 94) that even grandma would be proud of. To make a marmalade that is a bit more upbeat, try Mango (page 91) or Lemon Ginger Zucchini (page 90).

List of Recipes: Marmalades

Tomato sauce

Strawberry jelly

Marinated olives

Tomatoes and peppers

Blackberry jam

Cranberry jam

Traditional English Seville Marmalade

Don't be put off by the taste of fresh Seville-type oranges. Because of its high acid content, the Seville is not an eating orange. Yet its bitterness is magically transformed into a traditional English-style marmalade. Seville-type oranges are generally available in January and February, so mark your calendar to make a batch or two to enjoy throughout the year.

4	Seville-type oranges	4
2	lemons, very thinly sliced	2
4 cups	water	1 L
¼ tsp	baking soda	1 mL
4 cups	granulated sugar	1 L

1. Remove thin outer rind from oranges with vegetable peeler and cut into fine strips with scissors or sharp knife; or use a zester. Place rind, lemons and water in a very large stainless steel or enamel saucepan. Bring to a boil over high heat, cover, reduce heat and boil gently for 25 minutes, stirring occasionally.

2. Remove and discard remaining white rind from oranges. Cut oranges in half. Working over a bowl to catch juices, remove seeds with a sharp knife or fork. Place orange halves and juice in a food processor or blender and process until finely chopped.

3. Add chopped pulp and baking soda to lemon mixture in saucepan. Bring to a boil over high heat, reduce heat, cover and boil gently for 20 minutes, stirring frequently.

4. Add sugar to fruit mixture. Return to a boil and boil rapidly, uncovered, until mixture will form a gel (see page 23), about 20 minutes, stirring frequently. Remove from heat.

5. Ladle into hot jars and process for 10 minutes as directed on page 14 (Easy Step-by-Step Preserving).

Makes about 6½ cups (1.625 L).

Blueberry Orange Marmalade

Blueberries and citrus enhanced with a hint of cinnamon make this marmalade quite unusual. The recipe is adapted from one developed by the Wild Blueberry Producers Association of Nova Scotia.

1	small orange	1
1	lemon	1
2 cups	water	500 mL
1	cinnamon stick, about 3 inches (7.5 cm) long	1
2 cups	fresh or frozen wild blueberries	500 mL
2 cups	granulated sugar	500 mL

1. Squeeze juice from orange and lemon, including any pulp. Discard seeds and set juice aside. Slice rinds into very thin slices. Place rinds, water and cinnamon in a large stainless steel or enamel saucepan. Bring to a boil over high heat, reduce heat, cover and boil gently for 25 minutes or until rinds are very tender. Remove and discard cinnamon stick.
2. Add blueberries and reserved juice; return to a boil, cover and boil gently for 10 minutes.Add sugar; bring to a boil and boil rapidly, uncovered, until mixture will form a gel (see page 23), about 15 minutes, stirring frequently. Remove from heat.
3. Ladle into hot jars and process for 10 minutes as directed on page 14 (Easy Step-by-Step Preserving).

Makes 3 cups (750 mL).

Blood Orange Port Marmalade

The intense colors of blood oranges and port wine combine to give this unique marmalade a beautiful deep ruby color. Use this marmalade as a baste for chicken or fish or invite it to the breakfast table.

2	blood oranges	2
1	lemon	1
1 cup	water	250 mL
½ cup	port wine	125 mL
1¼ cups	granulated sugar	300 mL

1. Remove thin outer rind from oranges with a vegetable peeler and cut into fine strips with scissors or sharp knife; or use a zester. Place in a large stainless steel or enamel saucepan. Squeeze juice from oranges, discarding rind and seeds. Add juice and any pulp to saucepan.
2. Squeeze juice from lemon and slice rind into thin slices. Add lemon juice, rind, water and wine to saucepan. Bring to a boil over high heat, reduce heat, cover and boil gently for 30 minutes.
3. Add sugar, bring to a boil and boil rapidly, uncovered, until mixture will form a gel (see page 23), about 15 minutes, stirring frequently. Remove from heat.
4. Ladle into hot jars and process for 10 minutes as directed on page 14 (Easy Step-by-Step Preserving).

Makes 2 cups (500 mL).

Makes about 1¼ cups (300 mL).

Cranberry Orange Marmalade

The shiny scarlet cranberry lends a tartness to complement the orange of this marmalade. Make this marmalade when cranberries are at their peak between Thanksgiving and Christmas. But since cranberries freeze well, you can also make this marmalade year round.

2	medium oranges	2
1	lemon	1
3 cups	water	750 mL
2 cups	fresh or frozen cranberries	500 mL
4 cups	granulated sugar	1 L

1. Remove thin outer rind from oranges and lemon with vegetable peeler and cut into very fine strips with scissors or sharp knife; or use a zester. Place rind and water in a large stainless steel or enamel saucepan. Bring to a boil over high heat, cover, reduce heat and boil gently for 20 minutes.
2. Remove and discard remaining white rind and seeds from oranges and lemon. Finely chop pulp and cranberries in a food processor or blender and add to saucepan. Bring to a boil over high heat; reduce heat, cover and boil gently for 10 minutes, stirring occasionally.
3. Add sugar to fruit mixture. Return to a boil over high heat and boil rapidly,uncovered, until mixture will form a gel (see page 23), about 20 minutes, stirring frequently. Remove from heat.
4. Ladle into hot jars and process for 10 minutes as directed on page 14 (Easy Step-by-Step Preserving).

Makes about 5 cups (1.25 L).

Fresh Mandarin Orange Marmalade

This delicate, fresh-tasting orange marmalade appeals to those who dislike the intense flavor of traditional marmalades. Clementines, close cousins to the mandarin orange, are often less expensive and just as flavorful. The Fresh Mandarin Orange Cranberry Marmalade (below) makes a festive holiday spread and an attractive gift.

3	mandarin or clementine oranges	3
1	lemon	1
1 cup	water	250 mL
1¾ cups	granulated sugar	425 mL

1. Remove peel from oranges and slice thinly. Place in a small stainless steel or enamel saucepan. Remove thin outer rind from lemon with a vegetable peeler and cut into fine strips with scissors or sharp knife; or use a zester. Add rind and water to saucepan. Bring to a boil over high heat, reduce heat, cover and boil gently for 20 minutes.
2. Remove and discard white rind and seeds from lemon. Chop orange and lemon pulp finely in a food processor or with a sharp knife. Add to saucepan, return to a boil, cover and boil gently for 20 minutes.
3. Add sugar, return to a boil and boil rapidly, uncovered, until mixture will form a gel (see page 23), about 10 minutes, stirring frequently. Remove from heat.
4. Ladle into hot jars and process for 10 minutes as directed on page 14 (Easy Step-by-Step Preserving).

Makes 2 cups (500 mL).

Brandied Processor Grapefruit Marmalade

Imagine making a marmalade with no chopping or slicing! Just place all the fruit in a food processor and process. A splash of brandy and you have a gourmet spread that is an ideal gift.

2	small grapefruit (about ½ lb/250 g each)	2
1	lemon	1
2½ cups	water	625 mL
3¾ cups	granulated sugar	925 mL
2 tbsp	brandy	25 mL

1. Cut grapefruit and lemon into large pieces. Remove seeds and place in a tea ball or tie in a square of cheesecloth; set aside. Place fruit in a food processor and pulse until very finely chopped. You should have 2½ cups (625 mL) chopped fruit.
2. Place fruit and seeds in a large stainless steel or enamel saucepan. Add water, bring to a boil over high heat, reduce heat, cover and boil gently for 25 minutes. Remove and discard seeds.
3. Add sugar and bring to a full boil and boil rapidly, uncovered, until mixture will form a gel (see page 23), about 20 minutes, stirring frequently. Remove from heat and stir in brandy.
4. Ladle into hot jars and process for 10 minutes as directed on page 14 (Easy Step-by-Step Preserving).

Makes 4 cups (1 L).

Ruby-Red Grapefruit Marmalade

Eat your grapefruit on your toast? You certainly can with this grapefruit marmalade. The ruby-red fruit makes a delicious and attractive delicate pink marmalade.

3	pink grapefruit	3
2	lemons	2
3 cups	water	750 mL
3½ cups	granulated sugar	875 mL

1. Remove thin outer rind from grapefruit and lemons with vegetable peeler and cut into fine strips with scissors or sharp knife; or use a zester. Place rind and water in a large stainless steel or enamel saucepan. Bring to a boil over high heat; cover, reduce heat and boil gently for 20 minutes.
2. Remove and discard remaining white rind and seeds from fruit. Finely chop pulp in a food processor or blender and add to saucepan. Bring to a boil over high heat, reduce heat, cover and boil gently for 10 minutes, stirring frequently.
3. Add sugar to fruit. Return to a boil over high heat and boil rapidly, uncovered, until mixture will form a gel (see page 23), about 30 minutes, stirring frequently. Remove from heat.
4. Ladle into hot jars and process for 10 minutes as directed on page 14 (Easy Step-by-Step Preserving).

Makes 4½ cups (1.125 L).

Tangerine Grapefruit Marmalade

Tangerines, grapefruit and lemons give this tangy marmalade its unique flavor. As with many marmalades, this one may require several days to set.

2	tangerines	2
2	lemons	2
1	small grapefruit	1
3 cups	water	750 mL
2½ cups	granulated sugar	625 mL

1. Peel tangerines and slice rind thinly. Place rind in a large stainless steel or enamel saucepan. Remove thin outer rind from lemons and grapefruit with a vegetable peeler and cut into fine strips with scissors or sharp knife; or use a zester. Add to saucepan. Remove and discard thick white rind from grapefruit and lemons.
2. Cut all fruit pulp into large pieces and remove all seeds, being careful to catch all juice. Finely chop all fruit pulp in a food processor or blender and reserve. Place seeds in a tea ball or tie in a square of cheesecloth and add to saucepan. Add water, bring to a boil over high heat, reduce heat, cover and boil gently for 20 minutes.
3. Add reserved fruit pulp to saucepan and return to a boil. Cover and boil gently for 20 minutes. Remove and discard seeds.
4. Add sugar to saucepan and return to a boil; boil rapidly, uncovered, until mixture will form a gel (see page 23), about 15 minutes, stirring frequently. Remove from heat.
5. Ladle into hot jars and process for 10 minutes as directed on page 14 (Easy Step-by-Step Preserving).

Makes 3½ cups (875 mL).

Five Fruit Marmalade

In early winter when honey tangerines, grapefruit, lemons, limes
and sweet oranges are at their best, make this tangy variation of a
traditional marmalade. Don't just eat it at breakfast. Try it as a glaze
on chicken breasts, baked ham and roasted pork.

2	lemons	2
2	limes	2
2–3	medium oranges	2–3
1	grapefruit	1
2	tangerines, peeled	2
4 cups	water	1 L
¼ tsp	baking soda	1 mL
5½ cups	granulated sugar	1.375 L

1. Remove thin outer rind from lemons, limes, 2 oranges and grapefruit
   with vegetable peeler and cut into fine strips with scissors or sharp
   knife; or use a zester. Place in a very large stainless steel or enamel
   saucepan. Remove the white rind in large pieces from lemons, oranges
   and grapefruit and place in saucepan. Add water; bring to a boil over
   high heat, cover, reduce heat and boil gently for 25 minutes.
2. Remove and discard remaining white rind from limes. Finely chop
   all fruit pulp in a food processor or blender; it should measure
   4 cups (1 L). (Add the chopped pulp of the remaining orange if
   needed). Add fruit and baking soda to saucepan. Bring to a boil
   over high heat, cover, reduce heat and boil gently for 20 minutes,
   stirring frequently. Using tongs, remove and discard the large
   pieces of rind.
3. Add sugar to saucepan and return to a boil, stirring constantly. Boil
   rapidly, uncovered, until mixture will form a gel (see page 23),
   about 30 minutes, stirring frequently. Remove from heat.
4. Ladle into hot jars and process for 10 minutes as directed on page
   14 (Easy Step-by-Step Preserving).

Makes about 6 cups (1.5 L).

Lemon Ginger Zucchini Marmalade

Fresh ginger combines with lemon to give a magnificent zing to this
marmalade. It's a nice change from the sweeter types. Chop the
ginger finely for a stronger flavor.

3	lemons	3
1	medium orange	1
2½ cups	water	625 mL
½ cup	chopped fresh peeled gingerroot	125 mL
1 cup	shredded zucchini	250 mL
4½ cups	granulated sugar	1.125 L

1. Remove thin outer rind from lemons and orange with vegetable
   peeler and cut into fine strips with scissors or sharp knife; or use a
   zester. Place in a large stainless steel or enamel saucepan. Remove
   the remaining white rind in large pieces and add to saucepan.
   Stir in water and gingerroot. Bring to a boil over high heat, cover,
   reduce heat and boil gently for 25 minutes. Using tongs, remove
   and discard white rind.
2. Finely chop fruit pulp in a food processor or blender. Add pulp and
   zucchini to saucepan. Bring to a boil over high heat, reduce heat,
   cover and boil gently for 20 minutes, stirring occasionally.
3. Add sugar to fruit mixture. Return to a boil and boil rapidly,
   uncovered, until mixture will form a gel (see page 23), about 30
   minutes, stirring frequently.
4. Ladle into hot jars and process for 10 minutes as directed on page
   14 (Easy Step-by-Step Preserving).

Makes about 4½ cups (1.125 L)

Mango Marmalade

The exotic sweet-tart flavor of mango permeates this tropical marmalade.

2	lemons, very thinly sliced	2
2 cups	water	500 mL
2	mangoes, peeled and thinly sliced	2
2 cups	granulated sugar	500 mL

1. Combine lemons and water in a medium stainless steel or enamel saucepan. Bring to a boil over high heat, cover, reduce heat and boil gently for 25 minutes, stirring occasionally.
2. Add mangoes to saucepan. Bring to a boil over high heat, stirring constantly; reduce heat, cover and boil gently for 20 minutes, stirring occasionally.
3. Stir in sugar. Return to a boil and boil rapidly, uncovered, until mixture will form a gel (see page 23), about 15 minutes, stirring frequently.
4. Ladle into hot jars and process for 10 minutes as directed on page 14 (Easy Step-by-Step Preserving).

Makes about 3 cups (750 mL).

Pear Apple Ginger Marmalade

This unusual combination of pears and apples produces a very fresh-tasting marmalade.

2	lemons	2
1½ cups	water	375 mL
4 cups	sliced peeled pears	1 L
4 cups	sliced peeled apples	1 L
¼ tsp	baking soda	1 mL
4 cups	granulated sugar	1 L
3 tbsp	finely chopped Candied Ginger or crystallized ginger	45 mL

1. Remove thin outer rind from lemons with a vegetable peeler and cut into fine strips with scissors or a sharp knife; or use a zester. Place in a large stainless steel or enamel saucepan. Remove white rind in large pieces from lemons and place in saucepan. Add water; bring to a boil over high heat, cover, reduce heat and boil gently for 20 minutes.
2. Finely chop lemon pulp in a food processor or with a sharp knife. Add lemon, pears, apples and baking soda to saucepan. Bring to a boil over high heat, cover, reduce heat and boil gently for 20 minutes, stirring frequently. Using tongs, remove and discard the large pieces of rind.
3. Add sugar and ginger to saucepan. Return to a boil over high heat and boil rapidly, uncovered, until mixture will form a gel (see page 23), about 20 minutes, stirring frequently. Remove from heat.
4. Ladle into hot jars and process for 10 minutes as directed on page 14 (Easy Step-by-Step Preserving).

Makes about 5½ cups (1.375 L).

Fresh Pineapple Marmalade with Lemon

Be sure your pineapple is fully ripe to best enjoy the flavor of this wonderful marmalade. It should be slightly soft to the touch with a strong color and no sign of green.

2	lemons	2
2 cups	chopped, cored peeled fresh pineapple (about ½ pineapple) (*see Tip*)	500 mL
2½ cups	water	625 mL
3 cups	granulated sugar	750 mL

1. Remove thin outer rind from lemons with vegetable peeler and cut into fine strips with scissors or sharp knife; or use a zester. Place in a large stainless steel or enamel saucepan. Remove and discard remaining white rind and seeds.
2. Finely chop lemon and pineapple in a food processor or blender. Add fruit and water to saucepan. Bring to a boil over high heat, cover, reduce heat and boil gently for 20 minutes, stirring frequently.
3. Add sugar to saucepan, return to a boil over high heat and boil rapidly, uncovered, until mixture will form a gel (see page 23), about 35 minutes, stirring frequently. Remove from heat.
4. Ladle into hot jars and process for 10 minutes as directed on page 14 (Easy Step-by-Step Preserving).

Makes 3½ cups (875 mL).

tip | *Your local grocery store will likely carry fresh pineapple available already peeled and cored.* .

Old-Fashioned Tomato Marmalade

Tomatoes impart a delicate fresh flavor to this preserve that is unique among marmalades. It's John Howard's family recipe. A variation adds chopped gingerroot during the cooking for a marmalade that is extra-special served with chicken, pork or fish.

5 cups	coarsely chopped peeled tomatoes (about 2½ lb/1.25 kg)	1.25 L
2	large oranges	2
1	lemon	1
4 cups	granulated sugar	1 L

1. Place tomatoes in a very large stainless steel or enamel saucepan.
2. Halve and seed oranges and lemon. Finely chop fruit in food processor or blender and add to tomatoes. Bring mixture to a full boil over high heat. Slowly add sugar, stirring until sugar is completely dissolved. Return to a boil and boil rapidly until mixture will form a gel (see page 23), about 1 hour, stirring frequently. Remove from heat.
3. Ladle into hot jars and process for 10 minutes as directed on page 14 (Easy Step-by-Step Preserving).

Makes about 6 cups (1.5 L).

Variation:
Gingered Tomato Marmalade
Add 3 tbsp (45 mL) finely chopped peeled gingerroot during cooking.

Microwave Gingered Peach Marmalade

Ginger adds a peppery pungency to the fresh peach flavor of this delightful marmalade. Freezing peaches in season allows us to make this small-batch microwave marmalade in the winter when oranges and lemons are at their best.

1	medium orange	1
1	lemon	1
½ cup	water or white wine	125 mL
2 cups	finely chopped peeled peaches, fresh or frozen	500 mL
2 cups	granulated sugar	500 mL
2 tbsp	finely chopped Candied Ginger or crystallized ginger	25 mL

1. Remove thin outer rind from orange and lemon with a vegetable peeler and cut into fine strips with scissors or sharp knife; or use a zester. Place rinds and water in a deep 8-cup (2L) microwavable container. Microwave, covered, on High (100%), for 5 minutes, stirring once. Microwave on Medium High (70%) for 5 minutes.
2. Meanwhile, remove and discard white rind and seeds from orange and lemon.Chop orange and lemon pulp finely in a food processor or with a sharp knife. Add to rind mixture. Microwave, covered, on High for 5 minutes, stirring once.
3. Add peaches, sugar and ginger. Microwave, uncovered, on High for 6 minutes, stirring every 3 minutes. Microwave on High for 12 to 15 minutes or until mixture will form a gel (see page 23), stirring every 4 minutes.
4. Ladle into hot jars and process for 10 minutes as directed on page 14 (Easy Step-by-Step Preserving).

Makes 2½ cups (625 mL).

Pear Kiwifruit Lime Marmalade

The brilliant green flesh of the kiwifruit gives this intriguing marmalade its beautiful jewel-like color. The principal growers of kiwi fruit, New Zealand and California, have opposite growing seasons, giving us virtually year-round availability.

3	limes, very thinly sliced	3
2½ cups	water	625 mL
2 cups	chopped peeled pears (about 3 pears)	500 mL
2 cups	chopped peeled kiwifruit (about 9 kiwifruit)	500 mL
4½ cups	granulated sugar	1.125 L

1. Place limes and water in a large stainless steel or enamel sauce-pan. Bring to a boil over high heat, cover, reduce heat and boil gently for 20 minutes, stirring occasionally.
2. Add pears and kiwifruit. Bring to a boil over high heat, cover, reduce heat and boil gently for 10 minutes, stirring occasionally.
3. Add sugar, return to a boil over high heat and boil rapidly, uncovered, until mixture will form a gel (see page 23), about 35 minutes, stirring frequently. Remove from heat.
4. Ladle into hot jars and process for 10 minutes as directed on page 14 (Easy Step-by-Step Preserving).

Makes about 6½ cups (1.625 L).

chapter 4

CONSERVES

ONSERVES are jams garnished with nuts — walnuts, pecans, and almonds—and sometimes with dried fruits. Often more than one fruit is used to give a rich, flavorful spread. It generally isn't necessary to add commercial pectin, since many fruits in combination often produce enough natural pectin to form a light gel.

Most of the summer fruits, such as cherries and blueberries, as well as fall cranberries, apples, pears and plums, lend themselves well to conserves. In an earlier era, conserves were often eaten as a dessert. Today, they are more commonly enjoyed as either a dessert sauce or a spread. And, in some cases, they are served as a savory accompaniment to meats: Apricot Grand Marnier Conserve (page 100) is a delicious example.

Generally, conserves are made the same way as jams. When dried fruits are called for, it is best to soak them for anywhere from a few hours to overnight. They will swell and soften as they absorb water and give a much better final yield after soaking.

Softer, fully sun-ripened fruits are the best choice for fruit butters and are made by cooking fruit until it is very soft, and then purÄeing it in a blender or food processor. Sugar and often some spices are then added and the mixture cooked until very thick.

Fruit butters have that great creamy taste associated with their namesake—butter—but contain no fat. Like butter, they can be used in baking to partially or completely replace the fat. Served with nippy cheeses, like Cheddar or Stilton, and plain crackers, fruit butters become an easy snack or an elegant dessert. Some make fine accompaniments to savory dishes.

Curds, commonplace in an earlier day, are gaining in popularity as refreshing additions to other foods. The traditional lemon curd has been updated with less fat and a far easier microwave cooking method (page 116). Microwave Orange Curd with Candied Peel (page 117) is a wonderful variation of this traditional treat.

It is best to make fruit curds in small amounts to store in 1-cup (250 mL) jars. Curds may be kept refrigerated for 3 weeks, but their fresh taste fades quickly and they are better eaten sooner than later. Freeze them for extended storage, keeping them ready for a fast defrost before using as an easy dessert.

Serving Suggestions:

We think conserves are among the very best items for gift giving. They offer a special touch of luxury that makes them a bit more special than other spreads. Conserves can be served with a plain cookie and a piece of Brie or Camembert cheese for afternoon tea.

Curds are beginning to show up in fashionable restaurants. Fancy bakeshops are using them as fillings for meringue shells and spreading them between cake layers. And we love spooning a dollop on waffles for an easy dessert.

tip   *Wrap a jar in a seasonal fabric, tie with a ribbon and attach the recipe and you have a wonderful gift.*

List of Recipes: Conserves

Apricot Grand Marnier Conserve

A beautiful golden color, this conserve follows through with great apricot and orange flavors. Use as a savory accompaniment to meats, or to top piping-hot biscuits or crispy herb toast.

2 cups	diced dried apricots	500 mL
4½ cups	water	1.125 L
1	large tart apple, peeled, cored and chopped	1
1 tsp	finely grated lemon rind	5 mL
¼ cup	lemon juice	50 mL
4 cups	granulated sugar	1 L
⅓ cup	Grand Marnier liqueur (see Tip)	75 mL
½ cup	slivered almonds	125 mL

1. Place apricots and water in a large stainless steel or enamel saucepan. Cover and let stand for at least 4 hours or overnight.
2. Add apple, lemon rind and lemon juice. Bring to a full boil over high heat, reduce heat, cover and boil gently for about 15 minutes or until fruit is tender, stirring occasionally.
3. Add sugar to saucepan. Return to a boil, reduce heat and boil gently, uncovered, until mixture will form a light gel (see page 23), about 25 minutes, stirring occasionally.
4. Add liqueur, return to a boil and boil gently for 5 minutes. Remove pan from heat and stir in almonds.
5. Ladle into hot jars and process for 10 minutes as directed on page 14 (Easy Step-by-Step Preserving).

Makes 5 cups (1.25 L).

tip | *The dried apricots are soaked in water to soften them and obtain a better cooked yield.*
The Grand Marnier liqueur can be replaced with thawed frozen orange juice concentrate.

Maple Blueberry Conserve with Walnuts

Any kind of blueberries, especially wild ones, make a marvelous conserve. Combine this with the nectar of the maple tree and you have a real New England treat. Fold it into yogurt for a pancake or waffle topping, or just spread it on toast or muffins.

2 cups	fresh or frozen blueberries, crushed	500 mL
½ cup	water	125 mL
¼ cup	maple syrup	50 mL
1 tbsp	lemon juice	15 mL
1 cup	granulated sugar	250 mL
½ cup	raisins	125 mL
¼ cup	chopped walnuts	50 mL
½ tsp	each: ground allspice and ginger	2 mL

1. Combine blueberries, water, maple syrup and lemon juice in a medium stainless steel or enamel saucepan. Bring to a boil over high heat, cover, reduce heat and boil gently for about 5 minutes or until fruit is tender, stirring occasionally.
2. Stir in sugar and raisins. Return to a boil, reduce heat and boil gently, uncovered, until mixture will form a light gel (see page 23), about 15 minutes, stirring occasionally. Remove from heat and stir in walnuts, allspice and ginger.
3. Ladle into hot jars and process for 10 minutes as directed on page 14 (Easy Step-by-Step Preserving).

Makes 1½ cups (375 mL).

Variation:
Blueberry Honey
Another blueberry pleasure for morning toast.
Finely chop ½ cup (125 mL) blueberries in a food processor. Add 1 cup (250 mL) creamed honey and pulse until blended. Store in a tightly sealed container.

Makes 1⅓ cups (324 mL).

Brandied Cranberry Conserve

This spirited conserve with the bright taste of cranberries is adapted from a recipe given to Ellie by her professor at the University of Wisconsin, Dr. Maxine McDivitt, who has made the recipe for years to give as Christmas gifts to faculty and friends.

1	small orange	1
1	cinnamon stick, about 4 inches (10 cm) long	1
3	whole cloves	3
½ cup	water	125 mL
1 tbsp	lemon juice	15 mL
3 cups	cranberries, fresh or frozen	750 mL
1½ cups	granulated sugar	375 mL
⅓ cup	brandy	75 mL
¼ cup	slivered almonds	50 mL

1. Finely chop orange in a food processor. Combine with cinnamon stick, cloves, water and lemon juice in a medium stainless steel or enamel saucepan. Bring to a boil over medium-high heat, reduce heat, cover and boil gently for 10 minutes. Remove cinnamon and cloves.
2. Add cranberries and sugar. Return to a boil, reduce heat and boil gently, uncovered, until berries pop and mixture will form a light gel (see page 23), about 5 minutes, stirring frequently. Remove from heat and cool slightly; stir in brandy and almonds.
3. Ladle into hot jars and process for 10 minutes as directed on page 14 (Easy Step-by-Step Preserving).

Makes 3½ cups (875 mL).

Cranberry Port Conserve

In memory of a good friend, Jane Hope, a Toronto home economist, this recipe was inspired using one of our favorite festive-season fruits, cranberries. It makes a dandy gift any time of the year for serving with hot tea biscuits, game or poultry. We remember her again with this wonderful recipe.

4 cups	fresh or frozen cranberries	1 L
2 cups	granulated sugar	500 mL
¾ cup	port	175 mL
½ cup	finely chopped peeled orange	125 mL
⅓ cup	raisins	75 mL
¼ cup	chopped walnuts	50 mL

1. Combine cranberries, sugar and port in a large stainless steel or enamel saucepan. Bring to a full boil over high heat and cook, uncovered, until berries pop.
2. Add orange and raisins. Return to a boil, reduce heat and boil gently, uncovered, until mixture will form a light gel (see page 23), about 15 minutes, stirring occasionally. Remove from heat and stir in nuts.
3. Ladle into hot jars and process for 10 minutes as directed on page 14 (Easy Step-by-Step Preserving).

Makes 4 cups (1 L).

Variation:
Raspberry Honey with Chambord
A delightful fruit honey with toast.
Stir together ¼ cup (50 mL) sieved fresh or frozen unsweetened raspberries, 1 tbsp (15mL) Chambord or Raspberry Schnapps and 1 cup (250 mL) creamed honey. Store in a tightly sealed container.

Makes 1 cup (250 mL).

Kiwifruit Cranberry Conserve

Tart dried cranberries add a crimson touch to kiwifruit's cool green
color and subtle sweet-tart flavor in this attractive sweet-and-sour
conserve.

1¾ cups	finely chopped kiwifruit (about 8 kiwifruits)	425 mL
1⁄3 cup	water	75 mL
¼ cup	fresh lime juice	50 mL
¼ cup	dried cranberries	50 mL
1¾ cups	granulated sugar	425 mL
¼ cup	toasted pine nuts	50 mL
1⁄8 tsp	ground nutmeg	0.5 mL

1. Place kiwifruit, water, lime juice and cranberries in a medium
   stainless steel or enamel saucepan. Bring to a boil over high heat,
   reduce heat, cover and boil gently for 10 minutes or until fruit is
   tender.
2. Add sugar. Return to a boil, reduce heat and boil gently, uncovered,
   until mixture will form a light gel (see page 23), about 15 minutes,
   stirring frequently. Remove from heat.
3. Ladle into hot jars and process for 10 minutes as directed on page
   14 (Easy Step-by-Step Preserving).

Makes 2½ cups (625 mL).

Sour Cherry Hazelnut Conserve

Cherry pieces and hazelnut halves suspended in a ruby-red gel promise the rich flavors to come. Enjoy this conserve with toasted crumpets or English muffins at teatime.

4 cups	coarsely chopped pitted fresh or frozen sour cherries	
	(about 6 cups/1.5 L whole)	1 L
1	lemon	1
1	medium orange	1
⅔ cup	dry white wine	150 mL
3 cups	granulated sugar	750 mL
½ cup	halved hazelnuts (filberts)	125 mL

1. Place chopped cherries in a large stainless steel or enamel saucepan.
2. Remove thin outer rind from lemon and orange with vegetable peeler or zester, chop finely and add to saucepan. Remove and discard remaining white rind from lemon and orange; chop pulp into small pieces. Add pulp and wine to cherries. Bring to a boil over high heat, cover, reduce heat and simmer for 10 minutes or until fruit is tender.
3. Stir in sugar. Return to a boil, reduce heat and boil gently, uncovered, until mixture will form a light gel (see page 23), about 20 minutes, stirring occasionally. Remove pan from heat and stir in nuts.
4. Ladle into hot jars and process for 10 minutes as directed on page 14 (Easy Step-by-Step Preserving).

Makes 4 cups (1 L).

Island Papaya Pineapple Conserve with Rum

This conserve will remind you of a winter holiday somewhere in the tropics. (Usually nuts are added to conserves, but not always—this recipe is an example of the no-nut type.)

1	lime	1
2	papayas, peeled and finely chopped	2
½ cup	canned crushed pineapple with juice	125 mL
½ cup	water	125 mL
4	whole cloves	4
1	cinnamon stick about 4 inches (10 cm) long, broken	1
2½ cups	granulated sugar	625 mL
½ cup	chopped dried apricots	125 mL
2 tbsp	finely chopped Candied Ginger or crystallized ginger	25 mL
1 tbsp	rum	15 mL

1. Remove thin outer rind from lime with a vegetable peeler or zester, chop finely and place in a medium stainless steel or enamel saucepan. Remove and discard remaining white rind from lime; chop lime pulp into small pieces.
2. Add lime pulp, papaya, pineapple, water, cloves and cinnamon stick to saucepan. Bring to a boil over high heat, reduce heat, cover and boil gently for 10 minutes or until fruit is tender. Remove and discard cloves and cinnamon stick.
3. Stir in sugar, apricots and ginger. Return to a boil, reduce heat and boil gently, uncovered, until mixture will form a light gel (see page 23), about 25 minutes. Remove from heat; stir in rum.
4. Ladle into hot jars and process for 10 minutes as directed on page 14 (Easy Step-by-Step Preserving).

Makes 3½ cups (875 mL).

Gingered Pear Apricot Conserve

An adventure in fruit, nut and spice flavors, this conserve is great as a
tart filling or over ice cream.

1	large lime	1
4 cups	finely chopped peeled and cored pears (4 large pears)	1 L
½ cup	water	125 mL
2½ cups	granulated sugar	625 mL
½ cup	chopped dried apricots	125 mL
¼ cup	finely chopped Candied Ginger or crystallized ginger	50 mL
¼ cup	slivered almonds	50 mL

1. Remove thin outer rind from lime with vegetable peeler and cut
   into fine strips with scissors or sharp knife; or use a zester. Remove
   and discard remaining white rind. Finely chop lime pulp with a
   knife or in a food processor with on/off motion. Place lime rind
   and pulp in a large stainless steel or enamel saucepan; add pears
   and water. Bring to a boil over high heat, cover and boil gently for
   10 minutes or until fruit is tender.
2. Stir in sugar, apricots and ginger. Return to a boil, reduce heat
   and boil gently, uncovered, until mixture will form a light gel
   (see page 23), about 20 minutes, stirring occasionally. Remove
   from heat and stir in almonds.
3. Ladle into hot jars and process for 10 minutes as directed on page
   14 (Easy Step-by-Step Preserving).

Makes 4 cups (1 L).

Plum Conserve with Maple Syrup

This conserve is an outstanding example of using both maple syrup
and sugar to provide sweetness and a "hint" of maple flavor. Blue
plums are best to use in season, but other types may be substituted.

3 cups	chopped pitted plums(about 1½ lb/750 g)	750 mL
3 cups	chopped peeled cored apples (about 3 large)	750 mL
1½ cups	water	375 mL
1	cinnamon stick, 4 inches (10 cm) long	1
2 cups	granulated sugar	500 mL
½ cup	maple syrup	125 mL
	grated rind of 1 lemon	
1 tbsp	lemon juice	15 mL
¼ cup	chopped hazelnuts	50 mL

1. Combine plums, apples, water and cinnamon in a large stainless
   steel or enamel saucepan. Bring to a boil over high heat, cover,
   reduce heat and boil gently for 10 minutes.
2. Add sugar, maple syrup, lemon rind and juice. Return to a boil
   and boil rapidly, uncovered, until mixture will form a gel (see
   page 23), about 20 minutes. Remove from heat and stir in nuts.
3. Ladle into hot jars and process for 10 minutes as directed on page
   14 (Easy Step-by-Step Preserving).

Makes 5 cups (1.25 L).

Festive Peach Conserve with Hazelnuts

The fresh fruitiness of peaches contrasts with the texture and sweet, rich, nutty flavor of hazelnuts in this attractive conserve. Use either fresh or frozen peaches. We often find frozen peaches in bulk food stores or you may choose to freeze your own when fresh peaches are in season.

1	each: lemon and large orange	1
3 cups	finely chopped peeled peaches, fresh or frozen	750 mL
½ cup	water or white wine	125 mL
2½ cups	granulated sugar	625 mL
½ cup	golden raisins	125 mL
¼ cup	chopped candied cherries	50 mL
¼ cup	coarsely chopped hazelnuts	50 mL

1. Remove thin outer rind from orange and lemon with vegetable peeler and cut into fine strips with scissors or sharp knife; or use a zester. Remove and discard remaining white rind and seeds.
2. Finely chop orange and lemon pulp with a knife or in a food processor with on/off motion. Place rinds and pulp in a large stainless steel or enamel saucepan; add peaches and water. Bring to a boil over high heat, boil gently, covered, for 10 minutes or until fruit is tender.
3. Stir in sugar, raisins and cherries. Return to a boil, reduce heat and boil gently, uncovered, until mixture will form a light gel (see page 23), about 25 minutes, stirring occasionally. Remove from heat and stir in hazelnuts.
4. Ladle into hot jars and process for 10 minutes as directed on page 14 (Easy Step-by-Step Preserving).

Makes 3½ cups (875 mL).

Variation:
Festive Nectarine Conserve with Almonds
Replace peaches with same amount of chopped nectarines, and replace hazelnuts with sliced almonds.

Winter Dried Fruit and Nut Conserve

You will find this marvelous conserve fabulous with goose, turkey or chicken, duck and pork roasts. It reminds us of mincemeat, but for meats. We've been known to eat it with cheese and crackers also.

2	Granny Smith apples, peeled, cored and diced	2
2	winter pears, peeled, cored and diced	2
½ cup	finely chopped dates	125 mL
½ cup	raisins	125 mL
½ cup	dried cranberries	125 mL
½ cup	apple juice	125 mL
2 cups	lightly packed brown sugar	500 mL
3 tbsp	lemon juice	45 mL
½ cup	coarsely chopped pecans	125 mL
⅛ tsp	each: ground allspice, nutmeg and ginger	0.5 mL

1. Place apples, pears, dates, raisins, cranberries and apple juice in a large stainless steel or enamel saucepan. Bring to a full boil over high heat, cover, reduce heat and boil gently for 10 minutes or until fruit is tender, stirring occasionally.
2. Stir in sugar and lemon juice. Return to a boil, reduce heat and boil gently, uncovered, until mixture will form a light gel (see page 23), about 10 minutes, stirring frequently. Remove from heat and stir in nuts, allspice, nutmeg and ginger.
3. Ladle into hot jars and process for 10 minutes as directed on page 14 (Easy Step-by-Step Preserving).

Makes 3½ cups (875 mL).

Sweet and Chunky Apple Butter

This fruit butter makes a quick dessert. It's also a great snack on bread or toast. We have found preserving in 1-cup (250 mL) jars convenient, since this recipe calls for that amount of apple butter. But if you use larger jars, you'll have lots left for other uses.

2 lb	McIntosh apples, peeled and cored (6 large apples)	1 kg
2 lb	Granny Smith apples, peeled and cored	
	(4 large apples)	1 kg
1 cup	apple cider	250 mL
2 cups	granulated sugar	500 mL
2 tbsp	lemon juice	25 mL

1. Cut McIntosh apples into 1-inch (2.5 cm) pieces. Cut Granny Smith apples into smaller dice.
2. Combine apples and cider in a very large stainless steel or enamel saucepan. Bring to a boil over medium-high heat, stirring occasionally. Reduce heat and boil gently for 20 minutes or until mixture is reduced by half.
3. Stir in sugar and lemon juice. Return to a boil, reduce heat and boil gently for about 25 minutes or until mixture is very thick. There should still be some tender apple chunks remaining. Remove from heat.
4. Ladle into hot jars and process for 10 minutes as directed on page 14 (Easy Step-by-Step Preserving).

Makes 7 cups (1.75 L).

Variation:
Spiced Apple Butter
Add 2 tsp (10 mL) ground cinnamon and ½ tsp (2 mL) each ground cloves and allspice with the sugar.

Apricot Honey Butter

Spread this elegant ambrosia on English muffins, pancakes or waffles.
You'll never miss butter again!

2 cups	chopped dried apricots	500 mL
2 tbsp	grated lemon rind	25 mL
2 cups	water	500 mL
½ cup	lemon juice	125 mL
¼ cup	finely chopped Candied Ginger	
	or crystallized ginger	50 mL
⅔ cup	liquid honey	150 mL

1. Combine apricots, lemon rind, water, lemon juice and ginger in a
   medium stainless steel or enamel saucepan. Bring to a boil over
   high heat, cover, reduce heat and boil gently for 35 minutes or
   until apricots are tender, stirring frequently.
2. Place apricot mixture in a food processor or blender and process
   until smooth; return to saucepan. Stir in honey. Return to a boil,
   reduce heat and boil gently, uncovered, until mixture is very thick,
   stirring frequently.
3. Ladle into hot jars and process for 10 minutes as directed on
   page 14 (Easy Step-by-Step Preserving).

Makes 2 cups (500 mL).

Cranberry Maple Butter

Use this thick ruby-red preserve as a filling for cakes or over pancakes, fresh fruits or ice cream as well as a fat replacement in muffins.

1 lb	cranberries (about 5 cups/1.25 L)	500 g
½ cup	apple juice	125 mL
½ cup	pure maple syrup	125 mL
¼ cup	liquid honey	50 mL
½ tsp	ground cinnamon	2 mL
1 tsp	vanilla extract	5 mL

1. Combine cranberries and apple juice in a medium stainless steel or enamel saucepan. Bring to a boil over medium-high heat, reduce heat, cover, and boil gently for 5 minutes or until cranberries pop, stirring frequently.
2. Remove from heat and purée mixture in a food processor until smooth. Press through a sieve and discard seeds. Return sieved mixture to saucepan; add maple syrup, honey and cinnamon and boil gently, uncovered, for 10 minutes or until thickened, stirring occasionally. Remove from heat and stir in vanilla.
3. Ladle into hot jars and process for 10 minutes as directed on page 14 (Easy Step-by-Step Preserving).

Makes 2½ cups (625 mL).

Spiced Plum Butter

The Shorter Oxford Dictionary defines plum as a "good thing ... the pick or best of a collection of things." This is an apt reflection of the high esteem held for the plum fruit. We think this recipe is a plum among butters. It works equally well with blue, red or purple plums.

10	plums, sliced	10
1 cup	water	250 mL
	granulated sugar	
1	cinnamon stick, about 4 inches (10 cm) long	1
4	whole cloves	4
½ tsp	ground nutmeg (optional)	2 mL

1. Place plums and water in a medium stainless steel or enamel saucepan. Bring to a full boil over high heat, cover, reduce heat and simmer for 20 minutes or until plums are tender, stirring occasionally.
2. Place plum mixture in a food processor or blender and process until almost smooth. Measure and return to saucepan. For each 1 cup (250 mL) plums, add 1¼ cups (300 mL) sugar. Tie cinnamon and cloves in a spice bag and add to saucepan.
3. Return plum mixture to a boil, reduce heat and boil gently, uncovered, until mixture is very thick, stirring frequently.
4. Discard spice bag; stir in nutmeg (if using).
5. Ladle into hot jars and process for 10 minutes as directed on page 14 (Easy Step-by-Step Preserving).

Makes about 3 cups (750 mL).

Variation:
Spiced Pear Butter
Replace plums with 5 peeled, cored and sliced pears.

Baker's Prune Butter

Butters are used in many ways. This one is best used as a fat replacement in chocolate cakes and brownies. Its dark color makes it most suitable for darker-colored baking.

1¾ cups	boiling water	425 mL
2	tea bags	2
½ lb	pitted prunes	250 g
¼ cup	granulated sugar	50 mL
1 tsp	grated lemon rind	5 mL
½ tsp	vanilla extract	2 mL

1. Pour boiling water over tea bags and steep for 5 minutes; discard bags.
2. Combine tea and prunes in a medium stainless steel or enamel saucepan. Bring to a boil over medium-high heat, reduce heat, cover and boil gently for 5 minutes or until prunes are softened. Remove from heat and purée mixture in a food processor or blender until smooth.
3. Return prune mixture to saucepan, add sugar and lemon rind, and boil gently, uncovered, for 15 minutes or until thickened, stirring occasionally. Remove from heat and stir in vanilla.
4. Ladle into hot jars and process for 10 minutes as directed on page 14 (Easy Step-by-Step Preserving).

Makes about 2 cups (500 mL).

Microwave Lemon Curd

Lemon curd has long been a staple in many English households. It is fast gaining popularity in North America as an easy dessert served in tart shells, as a filling for meringue shells or to spread between layers of a cake or on scones. Folded into whipped cream and layered with ladyfingers sprinkled with sherry, it makes a light and airy dessert. Making it in the microwave oven is much easier than making it in the traditional double boiler. Just be careful not to overcook it or it will separate.

2–3	lemons	2–3
¼ cup	butter	50 mL
¾ cup	granulated sugar	175 mL
2	eggs	2

1. Finely grate thin outer rind of lemons. Squeeze lemons. Measure ½ cup (125 mL) lemon juice into a 4-cup (1 L) microwavable container.
2. Stir in rind, butter and sugar. Microwave, uncovered, on High (100%) for 1½ to 2 minutes or until butter is melted and mixture is hot.
3. Beat eggs in a bowl. Gradually add hot lemon mixture to eggs, stirring constantly. Return mixture to the microwavable container and microwave, uncovered, on Medium (50%) for 1 to 2 minutes or just until thickened, stirring every 30 seconds. (Do not allow it to boil; mixture will thicken as it cools). Let cool.
4. Pour curd into a tightly sealed container. Refrigerate up to 2 weeks or freeze for longer storage.

Makes 1⅔ cups (400 mL).

Variation:
Lime, Tangerine or Orange Curd
Use 1 lime, tangerine or orange in place of 1 lemon.

Microwave Orange Curd with Candied Peel

Old-fashioned fruit curds are back in style! Adding candied peel to this orange curd makes it utterly mouth-watering. It is wonderful spread on scones warm from the oven. Making any curd in the microwave oven is so much easier and more foolproof than using the traditional double boiler. Just be careful not to over-cook the curd or it will separate.

3	**eggs**	3
2	**medium oranges**	2
1	**lemon**	1
¼ cup	**butter**	50 mL
¾ cup	**granulated sugar**	175 mL
⅓ cup	**candied orange peel, chopped**	75 mL

1. Beat eggs in a 4-cup (1 L) microwavable container.
2. Finely grate thin outer rind from oranges and lemon and reserve. Squeeze juice from oranges and lemon. Measure combined juice to give ¾ cup (175 mL) and whisk into eggs. Add rind, butter and sugar. Microwave, uncovered, on High (100%) for 2 minutes or until butter is melted and mixture is hot; whisk until smooth.
3. Microwave, uncovered, on Medium (50%) for 2 to 3 minutes or just until thickened, stirring every 30 seconds. (Do not allow it to boil; mixture will thicken as it cools). Stir in candied peel; let cool.
4. Pour curd into a tightly sealed container. Refrigerate up to 2 weeks or freeze for longer storage.

Makes 2⅓ cups (575 mL).

Variation:
Lime or Tangerine Curd
Replace 2 oranges with 3 limes or 2 tangerines.

chapter 5

LIGHT & LOW

S OME jams enjoy a less-sweet spread. Others make this choice for dietary reasons. In this chapter we offer ten spreads, so-called because they do not have enough sugar to be called a jam.

Some recipes call for powdered pectin for reduced sugar spreads that may be used with little or no sugar to make either cooked or uncooked spreads. This pectin is of special interest to those with diabetes or those who prefer a low-sugar breakfast spread, since they can also be used with artificial sweeteners. Unlike sugar, sweeteners do not affect formation of the gel. In recipes calling for sweeteners, you can reduce the amount up to a third to suit your personal taste.

This chapter has five recipes for cooked spreads and five for uncooked spreads. Except for Light Citrus Strawberry Spread (page 121), the cooked ones contain no added pectin and achieve their thickness from the natural pectin found in the fruits. They should be processed in a boiling-water canner. The uncooked spreads require added pectin, as do all uncooked spreads. They can be stored in the refrigerator for up to three weeks or in the freezer for longer storage. Be aware that spreads made with little or no sugar have a softer set than jams made with sugar.

Serving Suggestion:
Use these spreads as you would any jam. The nutrient analysis per serving is provided with each spread which will be of use to someone with diabetes.

List of Recipes: Light & Low

Light Blueberry Pineapple Spread

This all-natural fruit spread uses blueberries in an interesting combination with chopped orange, apple and pineapple juice concentrate, which provides most of the natural sweetness.

1	large orange	1
2 cups	blueberries, fresh or frozen	500 mL
1	tart green apple, peeled, cored	1
½ cup	frozen pineapple juice concentrate, thawed	125 mL
2 tbsp	granulated sugar	25 mL
2 tsp	lemon juice	10 mL
½ tsp	rum extract	2 mL
⅛ tsp	ground nutmeg	0.5 mL

1. Grate 2 tsp (10 mL) rind from orange; place in a medium stainless steel or enamel saucepan. Remove and discard remaining white rind from orange. Finely chop pulp in a food processor and add to rind.
2. Finely chop blueberries and apple in a food processor. Add to saucepan with pineapple juice, sugar and lemon juice. Bring to a boil over high heat, reduce heat and boil gently, uncovered, for about 25 minutes or until mixture is thickened and spreadable, stirring frequently.
3. Remove from heat and stir in rum extract and nutmeg.
4. Ladle into hot jars and process for 10 minutes as directed on page 14 (Easy Step-by-Step Preserving). Once opened, this spread is best kept in the refrigerator and used within 3 weeks.

Makes 2 cups (500 mL).

Nutritional Information per 1 tbsp (15 mL) serving
3 g carbohydrate, 0 g protein, 0 g fat,
0 g fiber, 0 mg sodium, 13 kcal (50 kJ)

Light Citrus Strawberry Spread

The diced orange helps extend the strawberries, particularly useful if you are using more expensive out-of-season berries. The tangy spread is quite refreshing. If you find it too tart, add liquid sweetener to taste.

1	large orange	1
4 cups	strawberries, washed and hulled	1 L
1 tbsp	lemon juice	15 mL
2 tbsp	granulated sugar	25 mL
1	box powdered pectin for reduced sugar spreads	1
1 cup	granular low-calorie sweetener	250 mL

1. Grate 2 tsp (10 mL) rind from orange; place in a large stainless steel or enamel saucepan. Remove and discard remaining white rind from orange. Chop pulp and place in a 4-cup (1 L) measuring cup.
2. Mash strawberries; add to orange. You should have 3 cups (750 mL) fruit.
3. Combine fruit, lemon juice, sugar and pectin in saucepan; mix well. Bring to a boil over high heat, stirring constantly. Stir in sweetener, return to a boil and boil hard for 1 minute, stirring constantly.
4. Ladle into hot jars and process for 10 minutes as directed on page 14 (Easy Step-by-Step Preserving). Once opened, this spread is best kept in the refrigerator and used within 3 weeks.

Makes 3 cups (750 mL).

Nutritional Information per 1 tbsp (15 mL) serving
3 g carbohydrate, 0 g protein, 0 g fat,
1 g fibre, 0 mg sodium, 11 kcal (50 kJ)

Light Strawberry Pineapple Spread

This all-natural fruit spread uses ever-popular strawberries and pineapple juice concentrate for most of its sweetness.

5 cups	strawberries, washed and hulled	1.25 L
1	Granny Smith apple, peeled, cored and chopped	1
1 tsp	grated lemon rind	5 mL
½ cup	frozen pineapple juice concentrate, thawed	125 mL
2 tbsp	granulated sugar	25 mL
2 tsp	lemon juice	10 mL
½ tsp	vanilla extract	2 mL

1. Mash strawberries in a medium stainless steel or enamel saucepan and measure; you should have about 3 cups (750 mL). Add apple, lemon rind, pineapple juice, sugar and lemon juice. Bring to a boil over high heat, reduce heat and boil gently, uncovered, for 20 minutes or until mixture is thickened and spreadable, stirring frequently.
2. Remove from heat and stir in vanilla extract.
3. Ladle into hot jars and process for 10 minutes as directed on page 14 (Easy Step-by-Step Preserving). Once opened, this spread is best kept in the refrigerator and used within 3 weeks.

Makes 3½ cups (875 mL).

Nutritional Information per 1 tbsp (15 mL) serving
3 g carbohydrate, 0 g protein, 0 g fat,
1 g fibre, 0 mg sodium, 12 kcal (50 kJ)

Light Spiced Raspberry Spread

This fresh-tasting spread uses a minimum of sugar and no sweetener.
Its sweetness comes mainly from apple juice concentrate and the
natural sweetness of the fruit.

3 cups	frozen unsweetened raspberries	750 mL
1	tart apple, peeled, cored and chopped	1
½ cup	frozen apple juice concentrate, thawed	125 mL
2 tbsp	granulated sugar	25 mL
1 tsp	grated lemon rind	5 mL
2 tsp	lemon juice	10 mL
⅛ tsp	each: ground ginger, cinnamon and nutmeg	0.5 mL
½ tsp	almond extract	2 mL

1. Mash raspberries in a medium stainless steel or enamel saucepan
   and measure; you should have 2 cups (500 mL). Add apple, apple
   juice, sugar, lemon rind and lemon juice. Bring to a boil over high
   heat, reduce heat and boil gently, uncovered, for 20 minutes or
   until mixture is thickened and spreadable, stirring frequently.
2. Stir in ginger, cinnamon and nutmeg; simmer for 3 minutes.
   Remove from heat and add almond extract.
3. Ladle into hot jars and process for 10 minutes as directed on page
   14 (Easy Step-by-Step Preserving). Once opened, this spread is best
   kept in the refrigerator and used within 3 weeks.

Makes 2 cups (500 mL).

Nutritional Information per 2 tsp (10 mL) serving
3 g carbohydrate, 0 g protein, 0 g fat,
1 g fibre, 1 mg sodium, 14 kcal (60 kJ)

Light Microwave Peach Plum Butter

This spread has great flavor and color with the thick consistency expected of a good fruit butter.

1 cup	finely chopped peeled peaches	250 mL
1 cup	finely chopped plums	250 mL
1 tbsp	water	15 mL
½ cup	granular low-calorie sweetener	125 mL
½ tsp	ground cinnamon	2 mL
¼ tsp	ground ginger	1 mL

1. Combine peaches, plums and water in a 4-cup (1 L) microwavable container. Microwave, uncovered, on High (100%) for 5 minutes, stirring once. Microwave, uncovered, on High for 10 minutes or until mixture is very thick, stirring every 3 minutes.
2. Stir in sweetener, cinnamon and ginger.
3. Spoon spread into clean jars or plastic containers to within ½ inch (1 cm) of rim. Cover with tight-fitting lids. Label jars and refrigerate for up to 1 week or freeze for longer storage.

Makes 1 cup (250 mL).

Nutritional Information per 2 tsp (10 mL) serving
3 g carbohydrate, 0 g protein, 0 g fat,
0 g fibre, 0 mg sodium, 11 kcal (50 kJ)

Light No-Cook Kiwifruit Pineapple Spread

Lime, along with pineapple juice, gives an interesting background flavor to the distinctive taste of kiwifruit in this easy-to-make spread.

1 cup	**finely chopped peeled kiwifruit**	250 mL
1 cup	**unsweetened pineapple juice**	250 mL
1 tsp	**grated lime rind**	5 mL
2 tbsp	**lime juice**	25 mL
1 cup	**granular low-calorie sweetener**	250 mL
2 tbsp	**granulated sugar**	25 mL
1	**box powdered pectin for reduced sugar spreads**	1

1. Combine kiwifruit, pineapple juice, lime rind and juice in a medium bowl; stir well.
2. Combine sweetener, sugar and pectin. Gradually stir into fruit. Let stand for 30 minutes, stirring occasionally.
3. Spoon spread into clean jars or plastic containers to within ½ inch (1 cm) of rim. Cover with tight-fitting lids. Label jars and refrigerate for up to 1 week or freeze for longer storage.

Makes 2¼ cups (550 mL).

tip | *Remember, the best flavor comes from fruit that is ripe but not too soft. Kiwifruit when purchased are often too firm. Wait for them to soften.*

Nutritional Information per 2 tsp (10 mL) serving
3 g carbohydrate, 0 g protein, 0 g fat,
0 g fibre, 0 mg sodium, 11 kcal (50 kJ)

Light No-Cook Mango Spread

For full-flavored "touch of the tropics" mango preserves, be sure the mango you choose is slightly soft to the touch. If not, keep it at room temperature for several days and check daily. Mangoes are ripe when they have a fresh, fruity aroma and yield slightly to gentle pressure.

2	large ripe mangoes, peeled and finely chopped	2
1 cup	unsweetened orange juice	250 mL
1 cup	granular low-calorie sweetener	250 mL
2 tbsp	granulated sugar	25 mL
1 tsp	grated orange rind	5 mL
½ tsp	ground nutmeg	2 mL
1	box powdered pectin for reduced sugar spreads	1
1 cup	water	250 mL

1. Combine mangoes, orange juice, sweetener, sugar, orange rind and nutmeg in a large bowl. Let stand for 10 minutes.
2. Gradually stir pectin into water in a small saucepan (do not add pectin all at once). Use a wire whisk or fork to mix well. Bring to a full boil over medium-high heat. Boil for 1 minute, stirring constantly. Gradually stir into fruit mixture. Let stand for 30 minutes, stirring occasionally.
3. Spoon spread into clean jars or plastic containers to within ½ inch (1 cm) of rim. Cover with tight-fitting lids. Label jars and refrigerate for up to 1 week or freeze for longer storage.

Makes 4½ cups (1.125 L).

Nutritional Information per 1 tbsp (15 mL) serving
2 g carbohydrate, 0 g protein, 0 g fat,
1 g fiber, 0 mg sodium, 9 kcal (40 kJ)

Light No-Cook Raspberry Pineapple Spread

Any fruit-based liqueur makes a nice addition to this fresh-tasting breakfast spread. The spread is excellent with English muffins or scones for afternoon tea.

4 cups	mashed raspberries	1 L
½ cup	unsweetened pineapple juice	125 mL
1½ cups	water, divided	375 mL
1 cup	granular low-calorie sweetener	250 mL
2 tbsp	granulated sugar	25 mL
3 tbsp	peach brandy or Cointreau	45 mL
1 tsp	grated orange rind	5 mL
1	box powdered pectin for reduced sugar spreads	1

1. Combine raspberries, pineapple juice, ½ cup (125 mL) water, sweetener, sugar, brandy and orange rind in a large bowl. Let stand for 10 minutes.
2. Gradually stir pectin into remaining water in a small saucepan (do not add pectin all at once). Use wire whisk or fork to mix well. Bring to a full boil over medium-high heat, boil for 1 minute, stirring constantly. Gradually stir into fruit mixture. Let stand for 30 minutes, stirring occasionally.
3. Spoon spread into clean jars or plastic containers to within ½ inch (1 cm) of rim. Cover with tight-fitting lids. Label and refrigerate for up to 1 week or freeze for longer storage.

Makes about 4 cups (1 L).

Nutritional Information per 1 tbsp (15 mL) serving
2 g carbohydrate, 0 g protein, 0 g fat,
1 g fiber, 0 mg sodium, 12 kcal (50 kJ)

Light No-Cook Strawberry Daiquiri Spread

A fruit spread version of the famous cocktail, its no-cook preparation gives it a really fresh taste. Also, it is possible to add liquid sweetener to suit your own taste.

4 cups	strawberries, washed and hulled	1 L
½ cup	unsweetened pineapple juice	125 mL
1 tsp	grated lime rind	5 mL
2 tbsp	lime juice	25 mL
2 tbsp	dark rum (optional)	25 mL
1½ cups	granular low-calorie sweetener	375 mL
2 tbsp	granulated sugar	25 mL
1	box powdered pectin for reduced sugar spreads	1

1. Crush strawberries in a large bowl; you should have about 2 cups (500 mL). Add pineapple juice, lime rind, lime juice and rum (if using). Stir well.
2. Combine sweetener, sugar and pectin. Gradually stir into fruit mixture. Let stand for 30 minutes, stirring occasionally.
3. Spoon spread into clean jars or plastic containers to within ½ inch (1 cm) of rim. Cover with tight-fitting lids. Label and refrigerate for up to 1 week or freeze for longer storage.

Makes about 3 cups (750 mL).

Nutritional Information per 1 tbsp (15 mL) serving
3 g carbohydrate, 0 g protein, 0 g fat,
1 g fibre, 0 mg sodium, 14 kcal (60 kJ)

Pancakes and strawberry jam

Beans and mushrooms

Wild leeks and mushrooms

Pickles

Pear Raspberry Jam

Homemade gifts

Light No-Cook Strawberry Kiwifruit Spread

Another fresh-tasting freezer spread that uses two very popular and available fresh fruits. Raspberries may be used to replace strawberries for a delectable variation.

3 cups	small ripe strawberries	750 mL
4	kiwifruit, peeled and diced	4
½ cup	unsweetened pineapple juice	125 mL
1½ cups	water, divided	375 mL
1 tsp	grated lime rind	5 mL
1 tbsp	lime juice	15 mL
1½ cups	granular low-calorie sweetener	375 mL
2 tbsp	granulated sugar	25 mL
1	box powdered pectin for reduced sugar spreads	1

1. Crush strawberries and kiwifruit in a large bowl; there should be about 3 cups (750 mL). Stir in pineapple juice, ½ cup (125 mL) water, lime rind and juice, sweetener and sugar. Let stand for 10 minutes.
2. Gradually stir pectin into remaining water in a small saucepan (do not add pectin all at once). Use a wire whisk or fork to mix well. Bring to a full boil over medium-high heat. Boil for 1 minute, stirring constantly.
3. Gradually stir into fruit mixture. Let stand for 30 minutes, stirring occasionally.
4. Spoon spread into clean jars or plastic containers to within ½ inch (1 cm) of rim. Cover with tight-fitting lids. Label and refrigerate for up to 1 week or freeze for longer storage.

Makes 3¼ cups (800 mL).

Nutritional Information per 1 tbsp (15 mL) serving
2 g carbohydrate, 0 g protein, 0 g fat,
1 g fiber, 15 mg sodium, 15 kcal (60 kJ)

Condiments

PICKLES, relishes, salsas, chutneys, mustards, ketchups—they all add the "spice of life" to our day-to-day meals. These savory, piquant, salty or spicy accompaniments are an easy way to make an otherwise ordinary meal special. Condiments are generally made by a pickling process. This process preserves the vegetable or fruit ingredients with an acid, usually vinegar. Good pickling technique is essential to creating great condiments.

Name That Condiment

Jams, preserves, jellies, marmalades, conserves and fruit butters all share the same characteristic consistency, thanks to a gel formed by pectin. What makes them different from one another is the size or absence of fruit pieces, the method of cooking and the addition of other ingredients. Fruit curds are unique because they are the only spread in this category thickened by eggs.

> **Pickle** is a piece of vegetable or fruit that has been preserved with a salt and/or a vinegar mixture. Pickles may be either sweet or sour and may use herbs or spices to provide extra heat and flavor.

> **Relish** is a pickle that has been chopped rather than left whole. Relishes can be sweet or sour, mild or hot.

> **Salsa** is a Mexican word for "sauce" and can be either cooked or fresh. It has come to refer to a blend of vegetables and/or fruits with spices and herbs.

> **Chutney** is a spicy condiment made from fruit, vinegar, sugar and spices. It originated in India, where it was known by the Hindu word *chatni*. Chutneys can be smooth or chunky and range in spiciness from mild to very hot.

Mustard is a sauce made from seeds of the mustard plant. Its spiciness ranges from mild to hot depending on the method of preparation and the variety of mustard seed. "Prepared" mustards are mustards mixed with other ingredients.

Ketchup is a spicy mixture made from the juice of cooked vegetables and fruits. In North America it is typically made from tomatoes.

Essential Pickling Ingredients

1. Vegetables and Fruits

Cucumber is the most common vegetable used in condiments. It is essential that cucumbers intended for pickling are not waxed. The thin coat of wax on the skin of the typical smooth green cucumber available in stores throughout the year prevents pickling brine from penetrating the cucumber. English seedless cucumbers are also unsuitable because of their very high water content. The smaller, squatter cucumbers with bumpy skins, sometimes called Kirbys, are the best cucumber for pickling. Remember to remove the blossom end of cucumbers before pickling. It contains enzymes that cause pickles to become soft.

Fruits as well as vegetables make interesting condiments. Whole pickled fruits add a tasty highlight to many meals. Many chutneys, salsas and relishes benefit from a variety of fruit flavors. Do not use frozen fruits or vegetables for making condiments, because freezing softens the texture. This affects the crispness and sometimes the flavor of the condiment. Whether vegetables or fruits are used, the best results come from the best produce. So choose the freshest and highest quality you can find.

2. Vinegar

Vinegar is the essential ingredient in the pickling process. It provides the acidity necessary to preserve produce as well as adding a piquant flavor. White vinegar is most commonly used because it does not affect the color of the condiment. Cider and malt vinegars do affect the color but are sometimes used for their interesting flavors. All our recipes are based on vinegars that have at least 5% acetic acid. Never use one with less. Check the label for the percentage, and avoid specialty vinegars as they often are lower in acid. Never reduce the amount of vinegar in a recipe. If you want a product that is less sour, add a bit of sugar instead.

The acid in the vinegar may change the color of some vegetables. All plant materials contain pigments, some of which are affected by acidity. One change frequently seen is the blue/green color that develops in garlic in a pickling brine. Don't worry—it is still safe to eat.

3. Salt

Salt affects both the flavor and texture of the finished condiment. It is important to use only pickling salt. Table salt contains iodine that can turn the condiment dark, as well as anti-caking agents that can give a cloudy appearance.

4. Sugar and Spice

Sugar is generally added for flavor, but it also helps to keep the preserved condiment firm. Most recipes call for white granulated sugar, but brown sugar and maple syrup may also be added for their flavors.

To maintain clarity of the pickling brine, spices added during cooking should be in their whole form. Either tie them in a small piece of cheesecloth or place them in a large tea ball for easy removal before processing. If you like a stronger spice flavor, add spices to the jar before packing the condiment ingredients. Ground spices are usually added to relishes and chutneys where clarity is not an issue. Always purchase spices in small quantities to keep them fresh, and store them in an airtight container away from heat, light and moisture. A spice rack over the stove may look attractive, but it is not a good place to keep spices fresh! (high pectin) to rhubarb (low pectin) or red currants (high pectin) to raspberries (low pectin) are good examples.

4. Acid

As well as having adequate pectin, fruit must contain the correct amount of acid to form a gel. Too much acid will form a gel that sets too quickly and too firmly, making the sweet spread "weep" as moisture is squeezed out. Marmalades often have too much acid so baking soda is added to reduce their acidity. Too little acid prevents a gel from forming so lemon juice is added to low-acid fruits to increase their acidity.

How To's of Pickling

The first step in pickling is either to sprinkle the vegetables with dry pickling salt or pour a salt brine (salt dissolved in water) over the vegetables. This draws out the moisture, resulting in a firmer product. The choice of method depends on the vegetable and the recipe. Soaking in brine requires more time but we find that generally it is the better method, especially for vegetables cut in pieces. It produces a less salty product than the dry-salt method. With either method, the soaked or sprinkled vegetable must be rinsed and drained to eliminate excess salt.

Preserving foods by pickling relies on exposing the food to an acid in the form of vinegar to discourage bacteria growth. The easiest way to do this is to pour a syrup made of vinegar combined with the salt, sugar or spices specified by the recipe over ingredients already packed into jars.

Condiments must be processed in a boiling-water canner. Grandmother may not have bothered, but it is absolutely essential to ensure the safety of your carefully made condiments. The heat produced by processing destroys the organisms that can grow in high-acid foods and spoil the product. The process also creates an airtight seal that prevents further contamination. The secret to crisp pickles is careful attention to pickling techniques and the right balance of the acid (vinegar) and salt.

chapter 6

PICKLES

PICKLING can be traced to India, over 4,000 years ago. Today, more than ever, we can revel in the marvelous versatility of pickles which is reflected in the variety of vegetables—and even a few fruits—in our recipes, including Madras Pickled Eggplant (page 158), which harkens back to the origins of this condiment.

North Americans are said to eat more than 20 billion pickles each year. The Japanese even eat them for dessert. While it will no doubt be a long time before the cucumber loses its popularity, we weren't surprised to learn that peppers account for more than 20% of specialty pickle sales. Fire-Roasted Pickled Sweet Red Peppers (page 155) are one of our favorite specialty pickle recipes since they have so many uses.

Many fruits and vegetables find their way into a pickle. Cucumbers, cauliflower and beets are favorites, but asparagus, sweet cherries and lemons offer interesting variety. Slightly less common, but in our opinion absolutely wonderful, are oranges, pumpkin and watermelon rind. All these can be made in sweet, sour or hot versions and flavored with such herbs as dill, mustard seeds, bay leaf, or peppercorns—the possibilities are endless.

Remember that you need perfect produce for perfect pickles. This means the very freshest produce available. Too long between harvest and preparation can result in hollowed or shriveled pickles. Most pickles need a few weeks to mellow before they are ready to eat.

Techniques for producing the perfect pickle

- Fresh produce is a must when making a batch of pickled anything.
- Always use pickling salt.
- Salt vegetables before making them into pickles. This draws out some of the moisture, producing a firmer pickle.
- Cut a thin slice from the blossom end of cucumbers to remove an enzyme that may cause pickles to soften.
- Process pickles in a boiling-water canner to destroy organisms that can cause pickles to soften.
- Check the label on vinegar to make sure that it has at least 5% acetic acid.
- Store prepared pickles a few weeks before sampling.
- Serve pickles cold and refrigerate pickles after opening.

Serving suggestions:

Pickles are a great way to add interest to just about any meal. They are a wonderful accompaniment to richer meats like pork and ham, helping to cut the fat taste. What self-respecting Rueben sandwich would adorn a plate without a kosher dill pickle? Any of our pickles make handy and welcome gifts, so make extra jars to give to friends.

List of Recipes: Pickles

Traditional Garlic Dill Pickles

An overnight stand in brine assures the crispness of these popular pickles. Use either small whole cucumbers or larger ones cut into quarters. For an additional interesting flavor, tuck a small dried hot chile pepper into each jar.

16–20	small pickling cucumbers (about 3 lb/1.5 kg)	16–20
8 cups	water	2 L
¼ cup	pickling salt	50 mL
2 cups	white vinegar	500 mL
2 cups	water	500 mL
2 tbsp	pickling salt	25 mL
4	large heads fresh dill or 2 tbsp (25 mL) dill seeds	4
4	small cloves garlic	4

1. Cut a thin slice from the ends of each cucumber. Place cucumbers in a non-reactive container. Combine 4 cups (1 L) water and ¼ cup (50 mL) salt in a large bowl, stirring until dissolved. Add 4 cups (1 L) ice water and pour over cucumbers. Let stand for 12 hours in refrigerator or a cool place; drain and rinse under cold water.
2. Combine vinegar, 2 cups (500 mL) water and 2 tbsp (25 mL) salt in a large stainless steel or enamel saucepan and bring to a boil.
3. Remove hot jars from canner. Place 1 head fresh dill or 1½ tsp (7 mL) dill seed and 1 clove garlic in each 2-cup jar. Pack cucumbers into jars and pour boiling vinegar mixture over cucumbers to within ½ inch (1 cm) of rim (headspace). Process for 10 minutes for 2 cup (500 mL) jars and 15 minutes for 4-cup (1 L) jars as directed on page 14 (Easy Step-by-Step Preserving).

Makes 4 2-cup (500 mL) jars.

Favorite Dill Pickles

A touch of sugar rounds out the sharp taste found in Traditional Garlic Dill Pickles (page 137). These pickles are not soaked in brine overnight so can be quickly made.

16–20	small pickling cucumbers (about 3 lb/1.5 kg)	16–20
2 cups	white vinegar	500 mL
2 cups	water	500 mL
2 tbsp	pickling salt	25 mL
1 tbsp	granulated sugar	15 mL
4	large heads fresh dill or 2 tbsp (25 mL) dill seeds	4
4	small cloves garlic	4
2 tsp	mustard seeds	10 mL

1. Cut a thin slice from the ends of each cucumber.
2. Combine vinegar, water, salt and sugar in a large stainless steel or enamel saucepan and bring to a boil.
3. Remove hot jars from canner. Place 1 head fresh dill or 1½ tsp (7 mL) dill seed, 1 clove garlic and ½ tsp (2 mL) mustard seeds in each 2-cup. Pack cucumbers into jars and pour boiling vinegar mixture over cucumbers to within ½ inch (1 cm) of rim (headspace). Process for 10 minutes for 2-cup (500 mL) jars and 15 minutes or 4-cup (1 L) jars as directed on page 14 (Easy Step-by-Step Preserving).

Makes 4 2-cup (500 mL) jars.

Garlic may turn blue or green in the jar. Nothing to be alarmed about, it is only the effect of the acid on the natural pigments in the garlic.

Sweet Garlic Dills

Among pickle lovers, we're absolutely convinced that no other pickle is a greater favorite than the dill pickle. These crisp garlicky ones are a fine example.

12–16	small pickling cucumbers (about 3 lb/1.5 kg)	12–16
4	large cloves garlic	4
4	heads fresh dill or 4 tsp (20 mL) dill seeds	4
½ tsp	celery seeds	2 mL
2 cups	white vinegar	500 mL
1 cup	water	250 mL
½ cup	granulated sugar	125 mL
2 tbsp	pickling salt	25 mL
⅛ tsp	turmeric	0.5 mL

1. Cut a thin slice from the ends of each cucumber. Cut cucumbers lengthwise into quarters.
2. Remove hot jars from canner. Place 1 clove garlic, 1 head fresh dill or 1 tsp (5 mL) dill seeds and ⅛ tsp (0.5 mL) celery seeds into each jar; pack in cucumbers.
3. Meanwhile, combine vinegar, water, sugar, salt and turmeric in a small saucepan and bring to a boil. Pour boiling vinegar mixture over cucumbers to within ½ inch (1 cm) of rim (headspace). Process 10 minutes for 2-cup (500 mL) jars and 15 minutes for 4-cup (1 L) jars as directed on page 14 (Easy Step-by-Step Preserving).

Makes 4 2-cup (500 mL) jars.

Salt-Free Dills with Horseradish

This is the pickle for those who need to reduce their salt intake. Fresh grape leaves are used to produce the crispness traditionally obtained with the use of salt. Either wild or cultivated grape leaves are appropriate.

12–16	small pickling cucumbers (about 3 lb/1.5 kg)	12–16
1	3 x 1-inch (7.5 x 2.5 cm) piece	
	fresh peeled horseradish (*see Tip*)	1
2½ cups	white vinegar	625 mL
2 cups	water	500 mL
4	fresh grape leaves, washed	4
4	cloves garlic	4
4	heads fresh dill or 4 tsp (20 mL) dill seeds	4
2 tsp	mustard seeds	10 mL

1. Cut a thin slice from the ends of each cucumber. Cut horseradish into 4 pieces lengthwise, and reserve.
2. Combine vinegar and water in a saucepan and bring to a boil over high heat.
3. Remove hot jars from canner. Place 1 piece horseradish, 1 grape leaf, 1 garlic clove, 1 head dill and ½ tsp (2 mL) mustard seeds in each jar. Pack cucumbers in jars.
4. Pour boiling vinegar mixture over cucumbers to within ½ inch (1 cm) of rim (headspace). Process 10 minutes for 2-cup (500 mL) jars and 15 minutes for 4-cup (1 L) jars as directed on page 14 (Easy Step-by-Step Preserving).

Makes 4 2-cup (500 mL) jars.

tip | *Horseradish adds a bit of flavor, but if you can't find the fresh root, just leave it out.*

Curry Pickle Slices

All curry lovers will be happy with this interesting flavor variation to a traditional pickle.

8 cups	small pickling cucumbers	2 L
4	small onions, sliced	4
1 tbsp	pickling salt	15 mL
2½ cups	cider vinegar	625 mL
1⅔ cups	granulated sugar	400 mL
1 tbsp	curry powder	15 mL
2 tsp	pickling spice	10 mL
1 tsp	each: celery seeds and mustard seeds	5 mL

1. Cut a thin slice from the ends of each cucumber and cut into thick slices. Place with onions in a non-reactive container, sprinkle with salt and let stand for 24 hours; drain. Rinse twice and drain thoroughly.
2. Combine vinegar, sugar, curry powder, pickling spice, celery seeds and mustard seeds in a large stainless steel or enamel saucepan. Bring to a boil over high heat. Add vegetables and return just to a boil. Remove from heat.
3. Remove hot jars from canner. Remove vegetables from liquid with a slotted spoon; pack into jars. Pour liquid over vegetables to within ½ inch (1 cm) of rim (headspace). Process 10 minutes for 2-cup (500 mL) jars and 15 minutes for 4-cup (1 L) jars as directed on page 14 (Easy Step-by-Step Preserving).

Makes 4 2-cup (500 mL) jars.

Cucumber Pickles with Lemon

These pickles will find favor with those who don't like the sharp bite of most pickles. Fresh lemon juice gives a nice lift to the cucumbers.

2 lb	small pickling cucumbers	1 kg
1 tbsp	pickling salt	15 mL
1⅓ cups	white vinegar	324 mL
1 cup	granulated sugar	250 mL
⅔ cup	lemon juice	150 mL
1½ tsp	peppercorns	7 mL
½ tsp	whole allspice	2 mL
3	slices fresh lemon	3
3	cloves garlic	3
3	bay leaves	3

1. Cut a thin slice from the ends of each cucumber and cut into thick slices. You should have about 7 cups (1.75 L). Place in a non-reactive container, sprinkle with salt and let stand for 3 hours; drain. Rinse twice and drain thoroughly.
2. Combine vinegar, sugar, lemon juice, peppercorns and allspice in a large stainless steel or enamel saucepan and bring to a boil over high heat.
3. Remove hot jars from canner. Place 1 slice lemon, 1 garlic clove and 1 bay leaf in each 2-cup.
4. Add cucumbers to boiling liquid and return just to a boil, stirring constantly. Remove from heat. Remove cucumbers from liquid with a slotted spoon and pack into jars. Pour hot liquid over cucumbers to within ½ inch (1 cm) of rim (headspace). Process 10 minutes for 2-cup (500 mL) jars and 15 minutes for 4-cup (1 L) jars as directed on page 14 (Easy Step-by-Step Preserving).

Makes 3 2-cup (500 mL) jars.

Best Bread-and-Butter Pickles

Most of our grandmothers made their own versions of bread-and-butter pickles. If you yearn for this bit of nostalgia, try our favorite version.

4 lb	small pickling cucumbers	2 kg
4	small onions, thinly sliced	4
1	sweet green pepper, seeded and cut in thin strips	1
1	sweet red pepper, seeded and cut in thin strips	1
2 tbsp	pickling salt	25 mL
4 cups	cider vinegar	1 L
3 cups	granulated sugar	750 mL
2 tbsp	mustard seeds	25 mL
1 tsp	celery seeds	5 mL
½ tsp	turmeric	2 mL
¼ tsp	ground cloves	1 mL

1. Cut a thin slice from the ends of each cucumber and cut into medium thick slices, about ³⁄₁₆ inch (4 mm). Place cucumbers, onions and peppers in a non-reactive container, sprinkle with salt and let stand for 3 hours; drain. Rinse twice and drain thoroughly.
2. Combine vinegar, sugar, mustard seeds, celery seeds, turmeric and cloves in a large stainless steel or enamel saucepan. Bring to a boil over high heat. Add vegetables and return to a boil for 30 seconds or just until cucumbers are no longer bright green.
3. Remove hot jars from canner. Remove vegetables from liquid with a slotted spoon; pack into jars. Pour liquid over vegetables to within ½ inch (1 cm) of rim (headspace). Process 10 minutes for 2-cup (500 mL) jars and 15 minutes for 4-cup (1 L) jars as directed on page 14 (Easy Step-by-Step Preserving).

Makes 6 2-cup (500 mL) jars.

Nine-Day Icicle Pickles

Icicle pickles have a long tradition. You probably remember your grandmother making them. Don't let the nine days deter you. The steps are simple—the rewards are well worth the effort.

8 cups	small pickling cucumbers, 4 to 6 inches (10 to 15 cm) long	2 L
4 cups	boiling water	1 L
½ cup	pickling salt	125 mL
2 cups	white vinegar	500 mL
3 cups	granulated sugar, divided	750 mL
1 tbsp	pickling spice	15 mL

Days 1–3

- Cut a thin slice from the ends of each cucumber. Cut cucumbers lengthwise into quarters. Cut each quarter crosswise in half. Place in a large non-reactive container. Combine boiling water and salt; pour over cucumbers. Place a weight such as a plate on top of cucumbers to keep them submerged. Stir once a day for 3 days.

Day 4

- Drain cucumbers and discard liquid. Cover cucumbers with fresh boiling water. Replace weight and let stand for 24 hours.

Day 5

- Drain cucumbers and discard liquid. Cover cucumbers with fresh boiling water. Replace weight and let stand for 24 hours.

Day 6

- Drain cucumbers and discard liquid.
- Prepare a brine: combine vinegar and 1½ cups (375 mL) sugar in a stainless steel or enamel saucepan. Place pickling spice in a large tea ball or tie in a piece of cheesecloth; add to saucepan. Bring to a full boil over high heat. Pour over cucumbers and let stand for 24 hours.

Day 7

- Drain brine into a large saucepan; add ½ cup (125 mL) sugar. Bring to a full boil over high heat. Pour over pickles and let stand for 24 hours.

Day 8

- Repeat Day 7, adding ½ cup (125 mL) sugar to the brine.

Day 9

- Drain brine into large saucepan and add ½ cup (125 mL) sugar. Bring to a boil over high heat.
- Remove hot jars from canner and pack pickles into jars. Pour hot brine over pickles to within ½ inch (1 cm) of rim (headspace). Process 10 minutes for pint (500 mL) and 4-cup (1 L) jars as directed on page 14 (Easy Step-by-Step Preserving).

Makes 3 or 4 2-cup (500 mL) jars.

tip | *The secret to crisp sweet pickles is adding the sugar gradually during the brining process.*

Winter Salad Pickles

Make this pickle when all the fresh vegetables are plentiful. Keep lots
on hand for a quick wintertime salad.

2 cups	cauliflower florets	500 mL
1 cup	peeled pearl onions, or larger onions	
	cut into quarters	250 mL
1 cup	thickly sliced celery	250 mL
1 cup	sliced carrot	250 mL
1 cup	thickly sliced zucchini	250 mL
1 cup	yellow beans, trimmed	
	and cut into 1-inch (2.5 cm) pieces	250 mL
2	medium sweet red peppers, seeded and	
	cut into squares	2
3 cups	white wine vinegar or Herb Vinegar (page 265)	750 mL
1½ cups	granulated sugar	375 mL
1⅓ cups	water	324 mL
2 tsp	pickling salt	10 mL
⅛ tsp	paprika	0.5 mL

1. Combine cauliflower, onions, celery and carrot in a large bowl.
   Combine zucchini, beans and peppers in a separate bowl.
2. Combine vinegar, sugar, water, salt and paprika in a large stainless
   steel or enamel saucepan. Bring to a full boil over high heat. Add
   cauliflower, onions, celery and carrot and return just to a boil.
   Remove from heat and stir in zucchini, beans and peppers.
3. Remove hot jars from canner. Remove vegetables from liquid with
   a slotted spoon; pack into jars. Pour liquid over vegetables to
   within ½ inch (1 cm) of rim (headspace). Process 10 minutes for
   2-cup (500 mL) jars and 15 minutes for 4-cup (1 L) jars as directed
   on page 14 (Easy Step-by-Step Preserving).

Makes 4 2-cup (500 mL) jars.

Mixed Vegetable Mustard Pickles

This pickle is the original version of chow chow. This name has now evolved to refer to any mixed vegetable pickle or relish made with mustard.

4 cups	small pickling cucumbers (about 1¼ lb/625 g)	1 L
4 cups	cauliflower florets (about 1 small cauliflower)	1 L
1 cup	peeled pearl onions	250 mL
½ cup	pickling salt	125 mL
6 cups	lukewarm water	1.5 L
3 cups	granulated sugar	750 mL
½ cup	all-purpose flour	125 mL
3 tbsp	dry mustard	45 mL
1 tbsp	celery seeds	15 mL
1½ tsp	turmeric	7 mL
3 cups	white vinegar	750 mL
½ cup	water	125 mL

1. Cut a thin slice from the ends of each cucumber and cut into thick slices. Place cucumbers, cauliflower and onions in a large non-reactive container. Combine salt with lukewarm water, stirring until dissolved. Pour over vegetables and let stand for 24 hours; drain. Rinse twice and drain thoroughly.

2. Combine sugar, flour, mustard, celery seeds and turmeric in a large saucepan; stir until well mixed. Whisk in vinegar and water. Bring to a boil over high heat, stirring constantly, until smooth and thickened. Add vegetables and return to a boil for 30 seconds.

3. Remove hot jars from canner. Remove vegetables from liquid with a slotted spoon; pack into jars. Pour liquid over vegetables to within ½ inch (1 cm) of rim (headspace). Process 10 minutes for 2-cup (500 mL) jars and 15 minutes for 4-cup (1 L) jars as directed on page 14 (Easy Step-by-Step Preserving).

Makes 5 2-cup (500 mL) jars.

Easy Spiced Pickled Beets

Pickled beets have long been a favorite in our families. Tiny beets are the most attractive, but larger ones cut into pieces are just as delicious.

8–15	fresh beets (about 2 lb/1 kg)	8–15
2 cups	granulated sugar	500 mL
2 cups	white vinegar	500 mL
⅓ cup	water	75 mL
16	whole cloves	16
8	whole allspice berries	8
2	cinnamon sticks, about 4 inches (10 cm) long	2
2 tsp	pickling salt	10 mL

1. Trim beets, leaving 1 inch (2.5 cm) of stem and tap root attached. Place beets in a large saucepan and cover with water. Bring to a boil over high heat, reduce heat, cover and simmer for 25 to 45 minutes or until tender. Drain and rinse under cold water. Remove skins and cut beets into large pieces.
2. Combine sugar, vinegar and water in a large saucepan. Bring to a boil over high heat, stirring occasionally.
3. Remove hot jars from canner and place 4 whole cloves, 2 allspice berries, ½ cinnamon stick and ½ tsp (2 mL) salt in each jar. Pack beet pieces into jars.
4. Pour hot liquid over beets to within ½ inch (1 cm) of rim (headspace). Process 30 minutes for 2-cup (500 mL) jars and 35 minutes for 4-cup (1 L) jars as directed on page 14 (Easy Step-by-Step Preserving).

Makes 4 2-cup (500 mL) jars.

Pickled Beets and Onions

This pickled beet variation with caraway and mustard seeds adds new interest to a traditional favorite. Use tiny beets and onions for a pickle with a more elegant appearance. But larger ones cut into quarters work just as well.

10–15	small fresh beets	10–15
2 cups	cider vinegar	500 mL
1½ cups	granulated sugar	375 mL
½ cup	water	125 mL
1 cup	peeled small whole onions (about 4 oz/250 g)	250 mL
2 tsp	pickling salt	10 mL
2 tsp	caraway seeds	10 mL
1 tsp	mustard seeds	5 mL

1. Trim beets, leaving 1 inch (2.5 cm) of stem and tap root attached. Place beets in a large saucepan, cover with water and bring to a boil over high heat. Reduce heat, cover and simmer for 25 to 40 minutes or until tender. Drain and rinse under cold water. Remove skins and cut beets into serving-sized pieces if necessary.
2. Combine vinegar, sugar and water in a saucepan. Bring to a boil over high heat, stirring occasionally.
3. Remove hot jars from canner. Divide onions, caraway seeds and mustard seeds equally among jars; add beet pieces.
4. Pour boiling vinegar mixture over beets to within ½ inch (1 cm) of rim (headspace). Process 30 minutes for 2-cup (500 mL) jars and 35 minutes for 4-cup (1 L) jars as directed on page 14 (Easy Step-by-Step Preserving).

Makes 4 2-cup (500 mL) jars.

Lemon Spiced Bean Pickle

Green and yellow beans pickled with a bit of lemon are nice with cold meats or on a relish tray. Pack the beans into wide-mouth jars placed on their sides.

1 lb	green beans	500 g
1 lb	yellow beans	500 g
2½ cups	cider vinegar	625 mL
1¼ cups	water	300 mL
1 tbsp	pickling salt	15 mL
1 tbsp	granulated sugar	15 mL
1 tbsp	pickling spice	15 mL
3	strips lemon rind	3

1. Wash and trim beans into 4-inch (10 cm) lengths to fit into jars.
2. Combine vinegar, water, salt and sugar in a medium saucepan and bring to a boil over high heat. Add beans, cover and return to a boil; boil for 1 minute. Remove from heat and drain, reserving liquid. Return liquid to saucepan and bring to a boil.
3. Remove hot jars from canner and place 1 tsp (5 mL) pickling spice and 1 strip lemon rind into each jar. Pack in beans and pour boiling liquid into jars to within ½ inch (1 cm) of rim (headspace). Process 10 minutes for 2-cup (500 mL) jars as directed on page 14 (Easy Step-by-Step Preserving).

Makes 3 2-cup (500 mL) jars.

Herbed Asparagus Pickles

Tarragon appears in the spring just as asparagus begins to push out of the ground. The two combine to make a savory pickle that is quite out-of-the-ordinary.

2½–3 lb	asparagus spears	1.25–1.5 kg
4	sprigs fresh tarragon	4
2	small dry shallots, halved	2
2 cups	white wine vinegar	500 mL
1½ cups	white vinegar	375 mL
1 cup	water	250 mL
¼ cup	granulated sugar	50 mL
1 tsp	pickling salt	5 mL

1. Wash asparagus and cut each spear 4¼ inches (11 cm) long or long enough to fit a wide-mouth pint (500 mL) jar leaving ¾ inch (2 cm) headspace.
2. Remove hot jars from canner and pack asparagus into jars with tips down. Tuck a sprig of tarragon and half a shallot among the spears.
3. Combine wine vinegar, white vinegar, water, sugar and salt in a medium saucepan and bring to a boil. Pour boiling vinegar mixture over asparagus to within ½ inch (1 cm) of rim (headspace). Process 15 minutes for 2-cup (500 mL) jars as directed on page 14 (Easy Step-by-Step Preserving).

Makes 4 2-cup (500 mL) jars.

Pickled Baby Carrots with Oregano and Peppers

Take advantage of packaged tiny peeled carrots to make this easy and interesting pickle.

3 tbsp	finely chopped fresh oregano or	
	1 tbsp (15 mL) dried	45 mL
2 tbsp	each: seeded chopped sweet red	
	and green pepper	25 mL
¼ tsp	hot pepper flakes	1 mL
2	small cloves garlic	2
1 lb	peeled baby carrots	500 g
1½ cups	white vinegar	375 mL
½ cup	granulated sugar	125 mL
⅓ cup	water	75 mL
1 tsp	pickling salt	5 mL

1. Combine oregano, peppers and hot pepper flakes. Remove hot jars from canner and divide pepper mixture between them. Add 1 clove garlic to each jar and fill each with half the carrots leaving ½ inch (1 cm) headspace. (There may be a few carrots left over).
2. Meanwhile, combine vinegar, sugar, water and salt in a small saucepan and bring to a boil.
3. Pour hot liquid over carrots to within ½ inch (1 cm) of rim (headspace). Process 15 minutes for 2-cup (500 mL) jars as directed on page 14 (Easy Step-by-Step Preserving).

Makes 2 2-cup (500 mL) jars.

Carrot Zucchini Pickle Strips

Here is a neat pickle to make when zucchini are taking over the garden. Carrots and a hint of dill add interest.

1 lb	carrots, peeled and cut into short strips	500 g
1 lb	zucchini, cut into short strips	500 g
1 tsp	pickling salt	5 mL
1¾ cups	white vinegar	425 mL
⅔ cup	water	150 mL
⅓ cup	granulated sugar	75 mL
2 tbsp	chopped fresh dill	25 mL
2 tbsp	chopped fresh parsley	25 mL
½ tsp	each: freshly ground pepper and dried thyme	2 mL

1. Cook carrots in boiling water for 2 minutes; drain and refresh in cold water Combine carrots and zucchini; sprinkle with salt. Let stand for 4 hours; drain and rinse twice.
2. Mix vinegar, water, sugar, dill, parsley, pepper and thyme in a small saucepan. Bring to a boil, stirring until sugar has dissolved.
3. Remove hot jars from canner and pack vegetables into jars. Pour liquid over vegetables to within ½ inch (1 cm) of rim (headspace). Process 15 minutes for 1-cup (250 mL) jars and 20 minutes for 2-cup (500 mL) jars as directed on page 14 (Easy Step-by-Step Preserving).

Makes 5 1-cup (250 mL) jars.

Refrigerator Pickles

Thinly slice 1 unpeeled English cucumber. Layer ½ of cucumber with ½ thinly sliced small onion; repeat layers. In small saucepan combine ½ cup (125 mL) granulated sugar, ½ cup (125 mL) white vinegar, ¼ cup (50 mL) cider vinegar, pinch each: salt, mustard seeds, celery seeds and ground turmeric. Bring to a boil for 1 minute. Pour over cucumber and onion; let cool. Cover and marinate in refrigerator for 4 days. These crisp pickles keep in the refrigerator for up to 1 month.

Multi-Colored Ginger Pickled Peppers

Allow these pickles to sit for several weeks for the full flavor to
develop. Serve them with cold cuts or roasted meats and salads.

1	sweet green pepper, seeded and sliced lengthwise	1
1	sweet red pepper, seeded and sliced lengthwise	1
1	sweet yellow pepper, seeded and sliced lengthwise	1
2	jalapeño peppers, seeded and thinly sliced	2
1	2-inch (5 cm) piece gingerroot, peeled and thinly sliced	1
1½ cups	rice vinegar	375 mL
½ cup	water	125 mL
2 tbsp	granulated sugar	25 mL
1 tsp	pickling salt	5 mL

1. Place peppers and gingerroot in a shallow bowl. Combine vinegar,
   water, sugar and salt; stir well to dissolve. Pour over peppers.
   Cover and refrigerate overnight.
2. Drain peppers, reserving liquid. Remove hot jars from canner. Pack
   peppers into jars.
3. Bring drained liquid to a boil over high heat. Pour over peppers
   to within ½ inch (1 cm) of rim (headspace). Process 15 minutes
   for 1-cup (250 mL) jars as directed on page 14 (Easy Step-by-Step
   Preserving).

Makes 3 1-cup (250 mL) jars.

Radish Refrigerator Pickles

Combine ½ cup (125 mL) rice vinegar, 2 tbsp (25 mL) granulated
sugar, 2 tsp (10 mL) finely chopped gingerroot and 1 tsp (5 mL)
chopped fresh dill in a small bowl. Wash, trim and slice 2 bunches
radishes; toss with dressing, cover and refrigerate no longer than
2 hours before serving.

Makes 2 cups (500 mL).

Fire-Roasted Pickled Sweet Red Peppers

Roasted red peppers are fast becoming popular for everything from antipasto to pizzas, from garnishing a fresh mozzarella salad to enhancing a robust Italian spaghetti sauce. This recipe lets you roast peppers in the summer when they are plentiful to enjoy during the winter months.

6–8	small sweet red peppers (about 2 lb/1 kg)	6–8
1	large clove garlic, unpeeled	1
½ cup	dry white wine	125 mL
½ cup	white vinegar	125 mL
¼ cup	cider vinegar	50 mL
½ cup	coarsely chopped onion	125 mL
2 tbsp	granulated sugar	25 mL
½ tbsp	dried oregano leaves or1 tbsp (15 mL) fresh	7 mL
1 tsp	pickling salt	5 mL

1. Roast peppers and garlic on the barbecue grill or on a rack under the broiler until skins are blistered and starting to blacken. Place peppers in a paper bag until cool enough to handle; set garlic aside. When peppers are cool, remove skins, cores and seeds. Cut lengthwise into strips about 1 inch (2.5 cm) wide; set aside.
2. Combine wine, vinegars, onion, sugar, oregano and salt in a small stainless steel or enamel saucepan. Squeeze roasted garlic to remove from skin, mash and add to saucepan. Bring mixture to a boil over high heat, reduce heat and boil gently for 5 minutes.
3. Remove hot jars from canner and pack peppers into jars to within ¾ inch (2 cm) of top rim, being careful not to pack too tightly. Pour boiling vinegar mixture including onion to within ½ inch (1 cm) of rim (headspace). Process 15 minutes for 1-cup (250 mL) jars as directed on page 14 (Easy Step-by-Step Preserving).

Makes 4 1-cup (250 mL) jars.

Pickled Jalapeño Peppers

People who enjoy lots of heat with their meals will keep these preserved jalapeños for the time an extra spice accompaniment to a meal is needed.

1 cup	cider vinegar	250 mL
¼ cup	water	50 mL
4 tsp	liquid honey	20 mL
2 tsp	pickling spice	10 mL
½ tsp	pickling salt	2 mL
2	cloves garlic, halved	2
½ lb	jalapeño peppers, seeded and thinly sliced	250 g

1. Combine vinegar, water, honey, pickling spice and salt in a small saucepan. Bring to a boil over high heat, remove from heat and let stand for 10 minutes.
2. Remove hot jars from canner. Place ½ clove garlic in each jar. Divide peppers between jars. Add ½ clove garlic.
3. Return pickling liquid to a boil. Pour over peppers to within ½ inch (1 cm) of rim (headspace). Process 10 minutes for 1-cup (250 mL) jars as directed on page 14 (Easy Step-by-Step Preserving).

Makes 2 1-cup (250 mL) jars.

Mixed Japanese Pickle Sticks

Mirin, a sweet Japanese rice wine, gives these vegetable sticks an interesting flair. This low-alcohol golden wine adds flavor to a variety of Japanese dishes, sauces and glazes. It can be found in any Japanese market as well as the gourmet section of many supermarkets.

4	small zucchini, (about 1 lb/500 g)	4
4	medium pickling cucumbers (about 1 lb/500 g)	4
1	piece peeled Japanese white radish (daikon or lobok, about 1 lb/500 g)	1
2 cups	rice vinegar	500 mL
1 cup	water	250 mL
¼ cup	mirin	50 mL
2 tbsp	pickling salt	25 mL
16	black peppercorns	16
8	whole allspice	8

1. Cut zucchini, cucumbers and radish into lengthwise spears to fit into 1-cup (250 mL) jars or 2-cup (500 mL) jars. Set aside.
2. Combine vinegar, water, mirin and salt in a small saucepan and bring to a boil.
3. Remove hot jars from canner. Place 4 peppercorns and 2 allspice in each jar. Pack vegetables into jars. Pour hot vinegar mixture into jars to within ½ inch (1 cm) of rim (headspace). Process 10 minutes for 2-cup (500 mL) jars as directed on page 14 (Easy Step-by-Step Preserving).

Makes 4 2-cup (500 mL) jars.

Madras Pickled Eggplant

A friend of Margaret's daughter Martha, brought this wonderful family recipe with her from Calicut, India, when she came to live in Canada. It has unique Indian flavors that are quite delightful. Our only change has been to reduce the amount of oil.

2 lb	eggplant (2 large)	1 kg
3 tbsp	white vinegar	45 mL
2	large cloves garlic, minced	2
2 tbsp	chili powder	25 mL
2 tsp	each: ground ginger and turmeric	10 mL
¼ cup	canola oil	50 mL
1 tbsp	each: cumin seeds and fenugreek seeds	15 mL
1¼ cups	white vinegar	300 mL
1 cup	granulated sugar	250 mL
2–4	finely chopped seeded small hot red chile or jalapeño peppers	2–4
¼ cup	finely chopped gingerroot	50 mL
2 tbsp	pickling salt	25 mL

1. Cube unpeeled eggplant into bite-sized pieces and reserve.
2. Combine 3 tbsp (45 mL) vinegar, garlic, chili powder, ginger and turmeric in a small bowl to form a paste and reserve.
3. Heat oil over medium heat in a large nonstick skillet. Add cumin and fenugreek seeds and sauté for 1 minute. Add eggplant and sauté for about 10 minutes or until eggplant is just tender. Add reserved paste and 1¼ cups (300 mL) vinegar, sugar, chile peppers, gingerroot and salt. Stir over medium heat for about 5 minutes or until boiling.
4. Remove hot jars from canner and ladle pickles into jars to within ½ inch (1 cm) of rim (headspace). Process 15 minutes for 1-cup (250 mL) jars and 20 minutes for 2-cup (500 mL) jars as directed on page 14 (Easy Step-by-Step Preserving).

Makes 6 1-cup (250 mL) jars or 3 2-cup (500 mL) jars.

Pickled Ginger

Keep a jar of this easy-to-make pickle on your shelf to make speedy additions to stir-fries. Pickled ginger and its jalapeño and garlic variations also add zest to antipasto plates, meat loaf and any other dishes in need of a pickled spice lift.

1	large piece fresh gingerroot (about 10 oz/280 g)	1
¾ cup	rice wine vinegar	175 mL
½ cup	white vinegar	125 mL
2 tsp	soy sauce	10 mL
1 tsp	granulated sugar	5 mL

1. Peel ginger and cut into pieces no larger than 1 inch (2.5 cm). Remove hot jars from canner and pack ginger into jars.
2. Bring vinegars, soy sauce and sugar to a boil in a small saucepan. Pour over ginger to within ½ inch (1 cm) of rim (headspace). Process 10 minutes for 1-cup (250 mL) and ½-cup (125 mL) jars as directed on page 14 (Easy Step-by-Step Preserving).

Makes 2 1-cup (250 mL) jars or 4 half-cup (125 mL) jars.

Variations:
Pickled Jalapeños
Replace ginger with 10–12 jalapeño peppers, depending on their size. Omit soy sauce and add ½ tsp (2 mL) salt.

Pickled Garlic
Replace ginger with 3–4 heads garlic, depending on their size. Omit soy sauce and add ½ tsp (2 mL) salt plus 2 tsp (10 mL) pickling spice, if desired.

tip | *Fresh gingerroot may be frozen to have on hand to add to a variety of dishes. Cut in pieces and freeze in a tightly sealed freezer bag. When needed, the frozen gingerroot may be easily peeled and grated.*

Pickled Sweet Cherries

This unusual and colorful pickle with its sweet-sour taste makes an excellent condiment for game and poultry as well as other roasted meats.

1¾ cups	white vinegar	425 mL
1¾ cups	granulated sugar	425 mL
¾ cup	water	175 mL
2	cinnamon sticks, about 4 inches (10 cm) long	2
2 tsp	whole cloves	10 mL
1 tsp	whole allspice	5 mL
2 lb	dark sweet cherries with stems	1 kg

1. Combine vinegar, sugar, water, cinnamon, cloves and allspice in a small saucepan. Bring to a boil, reduce heat and boil gently, uncovered, for 20 minutes.
2. Remove hot jars from canner and pack cherries into jars. Pour hot syrup over cherries to within ½ inch (1 cm) of rim (headspace). Process 15 minutes for 2-cup (500 mL) jars as directed on page 14 (Easy Step-by-Step Preserving).

Makes 3 2-cup (500 mL) jars.

Variation:
Pickled Plums
Replace sweet cherries with red or blue plums. Process 20 minutes for 2-cup (500 mL) jars as directed on page 14 (Easy Step-by-Step Preserving).

Spiced Wine Peach Jam

Peaches

Spiced Pickled Peaches

Both the peach and the pineapple version of this condiment is a wonderful accompaniment to many meals. Look for very small peaches. If you can find only large ones, cut them into quarters.

21–24	small peaches (about 4 lb/2 kg)	21–24
3½ cups	granulated sugar	875 mL
1¾ cups	white vinegar	425 mL
1¼ cup	water	300 mL
3	cinnamon sticks, 3 inches (8 cm) long, broken	3
1 tbsp	whole cloves	15 mL
½ tsp	whole allspice	2 mL

1. Bring a saucepan of water to a boil over high heat. Dip peaches into boiling water for about 30 seconds or until skins will slip off easily. Peel peaches and place in a solution of 8 cups (2 L) water and 1 tsp (5 mL) lemon juice.
2. Bring sugar, vinegar and water to a boil over high heat in a large stainless steel or enamel saucepan, stirring until sugar is dissolved. Tie cinnamon, cloves and allspice in a cheesecloth bag; add to sugar. Reduce heat, cover and boil gently for 10 minutes.
3. Drain peaches and add to syrup. Return to a boil and boil gently for 5 minutes. Discard spice bag.
4. Remove hot jars from canner. Remove peaches from liquid with a slotted spoon; pack into jars. Pour liquid over peaches to within ½ inch (1 cm) of rim (headspace). Process 20 minutes for 2-cup (500 mL) jars and 25 minutes for 4-cup (1 L) jars as directed on page 14 (Easy Step-by-Step Preserving).

Makes 6 2-cup (500 mL) jars.

Pumpkin Pickles

This famous pickle comes from a friend of a friend. She suggests putting a light rather than a candle inside your Halloween pumpkin so you can recycle it into pickles. Better still, paint a face on the pumpkin with magic markers.

1	**large pumpkin (about 5 lb/2.5 kg)**	1
6 cups	**granulated sugar**	1.5 L
3 cups	**white or cider vinegar**	750 mL
1 tsp	**whole cloves**	5 mL
1	**cinnamon stick, about 4 inches (10 cm) long, broken**	1
2	**pieces Candied Ginger or crystallized ginger**	2

1. Peel pumpkin, remove seeds and cut into 2-inch (5 cm) cubes.
2. Bring sugar and vinegar to a boil over high heat in a large stainless steel or enamel saucepan, stirring until sugar is dissolved. Tie cloves, cinnamon and ginger tightly in cheesecloth bag; add to sugar. Reduce heat and boil gently for 5 minutes.
3. Add pumpkin pieces and return to a boil. Reduce heat, cover, and boil gently for 25 minutes or until pumpkin is tender but pieces still hold their shape, stirring frequently. Discard spice bag.
4. Remove hot jars from canner. Remove pumpkin from liquid with a slotted spoon; pack tightly into jars. Pour liquid over pumpkin to within ½ inch (1 cm) of rim (headspace). Process 20 minutes for 1-cup (250 mL) jars and 2-cup (500 mL) jars as directed on page 14 (Easy Step-by-Step Preserving).

Makes 5 2-cup (500 mL) jars.

 Depending on the size of the pumpkin, you may need to make more of the syrup. Always use the same proportions called for in the recipe: 2 parts sugar to 1 part white vinegar.

Spiced Orange Slices

We were served these unusual orange pickle slices on recent trips to Australia. They came as an accompaniment to a cheese tray. Since they are a sweet-sour condiment, they are not a traditional main course pickle.

4	large oranges	4
8 cups	hot water	2 L
1 tsp	salt	5 mL
1 cup	granulated sugar	250 mL
½ cup	lightly packed brown sugar	125 mL
½ cup	each: cider vinegar and water	125 mL
¼ cup	corn syrup	50 mL
8	whole cloves	8
4	cardamom pods	4
4	cinnamon sticks, 3 inches (8 cm) long	4
½ tsp	peppercorns	2 mL

1. Combine whole unpeeled oranges, 8 cups (2 L) hot water and salt in a large saucepan. Bring to a boil, reduce heat, cover and simmer for 45 minutes or until fruit is tender. Drain oranges, discarding liquid, and cool.
2. Cut oranges in half crosswise and then into very thin slices.
3. Combine granulated sugar, brown sugar, vinegar, water, corn syrup, cloves, cardamom, cinnamon and peppercorns in a large saucepan. Stir over high heat until sugars have dissolved. Reduce heat and cook for 10 minutes. Add orange slices, cover and cook gently for 20 minutes. Remove from heat and let stand for 5 minutes. Remove and discard cardamom and cinnamon.
4. Remove hot jars from canner. Remove orange slices from liquid with a slotted spoon; pack into jars. Pour liquid and whole cloves over oranges to within ½ inch (1 cm) of rim (headspace). Process 10 minutes for 1-cup (250 mL) jars and 15 minutes for 2-cup (500 mL) jars as directed on page 14 (Easy Step-by-Step Preserving).

Makes 4 1-cup (250 mL) jars.

Watermelon Rind Pickles

Make this delightful pickle from a part of the watermelon that is
often discarded. Leave a small amount of the pink flesh to give a bit
of color. Cut interesting shapes with canapé cutters. The secret of the
crisp texture is to add the sugar gradually during the pickling process.
The extra two days this requires is well worth the wait.

4 cups	peeled watermelon rind, cut into 1-inch (2.5 cm) cubes	1 L
¼ cup	pickling salt	50 mL
4 cups	water	1 L
2 cups	granulated sugar, divided	500 mL
1 cup	white vinegar	250 mL
1	lemon or lime, thinly sliced	1
1 tsp	whole cloves	5 mL
1 tsp	whole allspice	5 mL
2	cinnamon sticks, 3 inches (8 cm) long	2

Day 1

- Place watermelon rind in a large non-reactive bowl. Dissolve salt
  in the water and pour over rind. Let stand for 4 hours; drain and
  rinse twice.
- Place rind in a large stainless steel or enamel saucepan; cover
  with cold water. Bring to a boil over high heat, reduce heat, cover,
  and boil gently for 6 minutes, or just until tender. Drain; place in a
  large non-reactive bowl.
- Combine 1 cup (250 mL) sugar, vinegar, lemon slices, cloves,
  allspice and cinnamon in a saucepan. Bring to a boil, stirring until
  sugar is dissolved, and pour over rind. Place a weight such as a
  plate on top of rind to keep it submerged. Let stand for 24 hours.

Day 2
- Drain liquid from rind into a saucepan; add ½ cup (125 mL) sugar. Bring to a boil and pour over rind. Replace weight and let stand for 24 hours.

Day 3
- Drain liquid from rind into a saucepan; add ½ cup (125 mL) sugar. Bring to a boil. Add rind and return to a boil. Remove from heat.
- Remove hot jars from canner. Remove cinnamon sticks from liquid and place one in each jar. Remove rind from liquid with a slotted spoon; pack into jars. Pour liquid over rind to within ½ inch (1 cm) of rim (headspace). Process 10 minutes for 1-cup (250 mL) jars and 10 minutes for 2-cup (500 mL) jars as directed on page 14 (Easy Step-by-Step Preserving).

Makes 4 1-cup (250 mL) jars or 2 2-cup (500 mL) jars.

chapter 7

RELISHES

RELISHES have been around for so long that many have interesting histories. One of these is the chow chow relish. It is thought by some to have been created for Europeans residing in China. Another story has it that the chef to Napoleon developed the original chow chow relish and yet another that Chinese railroad laborers brought it to America. Whatever the origin, chow chow is a popular relish and we trust our Cauliflower Chow Chow (page 184) will win your heart.

Relishes are made from many different fruits and vegetables with added herbs and spices. It is best to chop the ingredients into equal-sized pieces so they have similar cooking times. And, like pickles, relishes should be processed in a boiling water canner.

All relishes in this chapter are cooked and then processed. Storage allows their flavors to mellow and continue to develop. For best flavor, allow relishes to wait a few weeks before tasting.

Relish ingredients with a high water content, like zucchini, onions and cucumbers, should first be put in salt water or layered with pickling salt to draw off some of their moisture. They are then drained and rinsed well before being cooked. Relish vegetables and fruits are cooked only until they are just tender to maintain their crisp texture. Most relish ingredients are available year round.

Serving suggestions:

Many great creamy salad dressings benefit from a spoonful of relish. Potato salad is also much tastier with a dollop of Sun Relish (page 178) stirred in. Did you ever consider adding some relish to a meat loaf? You may never again make one without! Try it with hamburger patties too.

And, of course, there is that combination of mustard and relish that transforms the lowly hot dog and hamburger.

The Antipasto Relish (page 169) is one of our favorites. The recipe contains directions for converting the relish to an antipasto by adding anchovies, tuna, olives and mushrooms at serving time. This is a very quick and convenient way to make an antipasto and eliminates the preserving problems associated with the low-acid nature of this condiment.

List of Recipes: Relishes

Antipasto Relish

This recipe becomes antipasto when you add tuna, olives, mushrooms and anchovies.

2	large cloves garlic, minced	2
¾ cup	white vinegar	175 mL
½ cup	each: water and tomato sauce	125 mL
¼ cup	granulated sugar	50 mL
2 tsp	pickling spice	10 mL
6	peppercorns	6
3	bay leaves	3
1 tsp	dried oregano	5 mL
1 cup	each: small broccoli and cauliflower florets	250 mL
¾ cup	bottled small pickled onions, drained	175 mL
½	each: large sweet red, yellow and green pepper seeded and diced	½
2	carrots, peeled and thinly sliced	2
1	jalapeño pepper, seeded and finely chopped	1

1. Combine garlic, vinegar, water, tomato sauce and sugar in large stainless steel or enamel saucepan. Tie pickling spice, peppercorns and bay leaves in a cheesecloth bag. Add spice bag and oregano to saucepan. Bring to a boil over high heat, reduce heat and stir until sugar is dissolved. Add broccoli and cauliflower florets, pickled onions, sweet peppers, carrots and jalapeño pepper. Return to a boil, reduce heat and boil gently for 1 hour or until mixture has thickened. Discard spice bag.

2. Remove hot jars from canner and ladle relish into jars to within ½ inch (1 cm) of rim (headspace). Process 10 minutes for 1-cup (250 mL) jars and 15 minutes for 2-cup (500 mL) jars as directed on page 14 (Easy Step-by-Step Preserving).

Makes 3½ cups (875 mL).

Apricot Red Pepper Relish

This gourmet relish is superb both as a topping to cream cheese spread on crackers and as a zippy complement to roasts.

1½ cups	cider vinegar	375 mL
1 cup	seeded and diced sweet red pepper	250 mL
¼ cup	drained Pickled Jalapeño Peppers (page 156)	50 mL
1¼ cups	chopped dried apricot halves	300 mL
3½ cups	granulated sugar	875 mL
1	pouch liquid fruit pectin	1

1. Combine vinegar, red pepper and jalapeño pepper in blender or food processor. Process with on/off motion until finely chopped but not puréed. Transfer to large saucepan.
2. Add apricots and sugar. Bring to a boil, reduce heat and cook for 5 minutes. Remove from heat and stir in pectin.
3. Remove hot jars from canner, and ladle in relish to within ½ inch (1 cm) of rim (headspace). Process 10 minutes for 1-cup (250 mL) jars and 15 minutes for 2-cup (500 mL) jars as directed on page 14 (Easy Step-by-Step Preserving).

Makes 5 cups (1.25 L).

Variation:
For extra spirit, add 2 tbsp (25 mL) port to mixture during cooking.

Green and Red Pepper Relish

We think this pepper relish is vastly superior to any commercial one. In fact, when sweet green and red peppers are in season, we always try to make our winter's supply.

4	sweet green peppers, seeded and chopped	4
4	sweet red peppers, seeded and chopped	4
4	medium onions, finely chopped	4
1 cup	white vinegar, divided	250 mL
1 cup	granulated sugar	250 mL
1 tsp	pickling salt	5 mL

1. Combine peppers, onions and ¾ cup (175 mL) boiling water in a large stainless steel or enamel saucepan. Cover and let stand for 5 minutes.

2. Drain vegetables and return to saucepan. Stir in ⅓ cup (75 mL) each vinegar and water. Bring to a boil, cover and reduce heat; simmer for 5 minutes.

3. Drain vegetables and return to saucepan. Heat remaining ⅔ cup (150 mL) vinegar, sugar and salt in a 2-cup (500 mL) microwavable container on High (100%) until sugar is dissolved. Add to vegetables and return mixture to a boil. Boil gently, uncovered, for 25 minutes or until liquid is reduced and vegetables are tender-crisp.

4. Remove hot jars from canner and ladle relish into jars to within ½ inch (1 cm) of rim (headspace). Process 10 minutes for 1-cup (250 mL) jars and 15 minutes for 2-cup (500 mL) jars as directed on page 14 (Easy Step-by-Step Preserving).

Makes 4 cups (1 L).

Barbecue Relish

This easy-to-make relish is so right with everything from hot dogs and hamburgers to egg salad or cold meat sandwiches.

4 cups	finely chopped zucchini (about 2 large)	1 L
1 cup	finely chopped onion	250 mL
1	medium sweet red, green or 1 yellow pepper, seeded and finely chopped	1
½ cup	finely chopped celery	125 mL
2 tbsp	pickling salt	25 mL
1½ cups	granulated sugar	375 mL
1¼ cups	white vinegar	300 mL
1 tbsp	celery seed, optional	15 mL
1 tsp	mustard seed	5 mL
½ tsp	each: dry mustard and ground cloves	2 mL

1. Combine zucchini, onion, pepper and celery in a large non-reactive bowl. Sprinkle with salt and cover with cold water; let stand for 1 hour. Drain vegetables in a sieve, pressing out excess moisture; reserve vegetables.
2. Combine sugar, vinegar, celery seed (if using), mustard seed, dry mustard and cloves in a large stainless steel or enamel saucepan. Bring to a boil over high heat; add reserved vegetable mixture. Return to a boil, reduce heat and boil gently, uncovered, for 45 minutes or until mixture is thickened.
3. Remove hot jars from canner and ladle relish into jars to within ½ inch (1 cm) of rim (headspace). Process 10 minutes for 1-cup (250 mL) jars and 15 minutes for 2-cup (500 mL) jars as directed on page 14 (Easy Step-by-Step Preserving).

Makes 3¼ cups (800 mL).

Beet Relish with Horseradish

Horseradish gives this savory beet relish extra zest to enhance any meat dish.

5	medium beets (about 1 lb/500 g)	5
1	large onion, finely chopped	1
2	sweet red peppers, seeded and finely chopped	2
1 cup	white vinegar	250 mL
½ cup	granulated sugar	125 mL
1 tsp	pickling salt	5 mL
⅔ cup	grated fresh horseradish	150 mL

1. Cook beets in boiling water until tender, about 20 minutes. Drain beets, remove skins and chop finely. There should be about 2 cups (500 mL). Mix beets with onions and peppers.

2. Combine vinegar, sugar, salt and horseradish in a large stainless steel or enamel saucepan. Bring to a boil over high heat. Add vegetables. Return to a boil, reduce heat and simmer, uncovered, for 20 minutes, stirring occasionally.

3. Remove hot jars from canner and ladle relish into jars to within ½ inch (1 cm) of rim (headspace). Process 15 minutes for 1-cup (250 mL) jars and 20 minutes for 2-cup (500 mL) jars as directed on page 14 (Easy Step-by-Step Preserving).

Makes 3½ cups (875 mL).

A can (14 oz/398 mL) of beets may be used in place of fresh for this relish.

Commercially prepared horseradish may be substituted for the fresh, but double the amount.

Cranberry Apple Pear Relish

The combination of apples and pears gives this versatile relish a lovely freshness as well as extending the cranberries. Orange liqueur and juice add a citrus flavor. We like using this relish with poultry or as an appetizer with crackers and Cheddar cheese.

3 cups	fresh or frozen cranberries	750 mL
3	apples, peeled, cored and diced	3
2	pears, peeled, cored and diced	2
1½ cups	golden raisins	375 mL
2 cups	granulated sugar	500 mL
1 cup	orange juice	250 mL
2 tbsp	grated orange rind	25 mL
2 tsp	ground cinnamon	10 mL
¼ tsp	ground nutmeg	1 mL
½ cup	orange liqueur	125 mL

1. Combine cranberries, apples, pears, raisins, sugar, orange juice and rind, cinnamon and nutmeg in a very large stainless steel or enamel saucepan. Bring to a boil over high heat, stirring frequently. Reduce heat and boil gently, uncovered, for about 25 minutes or until mixture thickens, stirring occasionally. Remove from heat and stir in liqueur.
2. Remove hot jars from canner and ladle relish into jars to within ½ inch (1 cm) of rim (headspace). Process 10 minutes for 1-cup (250 mL) jars, and 15 minutes for 2-cup (500 mL) jars, as directed on page 14 (Easy Step-by-Step Preserving).

Makes 6 cups (1.5 L).

Cranberry Rum Relish

Take this tangy cranberry relish to your next turkey dinner. We love it as an accompaniment to grilled chicken breasts and it is also splendid with pâté and crackers.

⅓ cup	dark rum	75 mL
¼ cup	finely chopped shallots	50 mL
	grated rind of 1 orange	
3 cups	fresh or frozen cranberries	750 mL
1 cup	granulated sugar	250 mL
½ tsp	freshly ground pepper	2 mL

1. Combine rum, shallots and orange rind in a medium saucepan. Bring to a boil over high heat, reduce heat and simmer for a few minutes until rum has reduced and mixture is a syrupy glaze.
2. Add cranberries and sugar. Stirring constantly, cook until cranberries pop and sugar is dissolved. Remove from heat and stir in pepper.
3. Remove hot jars from canner and ladle relish into jars to within ½ inch (1 cm) of rim (headspace). Process 10 minutes for 1-cup (250 mL) jars as directed on page 14 (Easy Step-by-Step Preserving).

Makes 2 cups (500 mL).

Easy Oven Relish

A fruity oven-prepared relish makes a delicious accompaniment to cold meats, meat loaves and roasts, and goes well with sandwiches.

3	large peaches, peeled, pitted and coarsely chopped	3
3	pears, peeled, cored and coarsely chopped	3
4	large tomatoes, peeled and chopped	4
2	large onions, finely chopped	2
1	large sweet green pepper, seeded and chopped	1
1	stalk celery, finely chopped	1
1½ cups	granulated sugar	375 mL
1½ cups	cider vinegar	375 mL
1 tbsp	whole allspice (tied in cheesecloth)	15 mL
1 tbsp	pickling salt	15 mL

1. Combine peaches, pears, tomatoes, onions, green pepper, celery, sugar, vinegar, allspice and salt in a large metal roasting pan.
2. Bring to a boil over medium heat, stirring occasionally. Transfer roasting pan to a 375°F (190°C) oven and bake, uncovered, for about 1½ hours or until mixture is thickened; stir occasionally. Remove from oven and discard allspice bag.
3. Remove hot jars from canner and ladle relish into jars to within ½ inch (1 cm) of rim (headspace). Process 10 minutes for 1-cup (250 mL) jars and 15 minutes for 2-cup (500 mL) jars as directed on page 14 (Easy Step-by-Step Preserving).

Makes 5 cups (1.25 L).

Fiesta Corn Relish

We especially like serving this colorful relish with cold meats and barbecued burgers. There is a hint of the Southwest in its flavors and its bit of heat. Frozen corn is almost as delicious as fresh corn, so this relish can be made any time of year.

5–6	Large ears fresh corn	5–6
1	hot yellow pepper, seeded and finely chopped	1
2	cloves garlic, minced	2
1½ cups	cider vinegar	375 mL
¾ cup	granulated sugar	175 mL
½ cup	chopped red onion	125 mL
½ cup	chopped sweet red pepper	125 mL
⅓ cup	chopped green onions	75 mL
1 tsp	ground cumin	5 mL
1 tsp	pickling salt	5 mL
½ tsp	freshly ground black pepper	2 mL
2 tbsp	chopped fresh coriander	25 mL

1. Bring a large pot of water to a boil over high heat. Add corn, cover and cook for 6 minutes. Drain and cool until easy to handle. With a sharp knife cut kernels from cob and measure 4 cups (1 L) corn into a large stainless steel or enamel saucepan.
2. Add hot pepper, garlic, vinegar, sugar, onion, red pepper, green onions, cumin, salt and black pepper to saucepan. Bring to a boil over high heat, reduce heat and boil gently, uncovered, for 20 minutes. Stir in coriander and cook 2 minutes longer. Remove from heat.
3. Remove hot jars from canner and ladle relish into jars to within ½ inch (1 cm) of rim (headspace). Process 15 minutes for 1-cup (250 mL) jars and 2-cup (500 mL) jars as directed on page 14 (Easy Step-by-Step Preserving).

Makes 4½ cups (1.125 L).

Sun Relish

Combining peaches and yellow peppers gives this relish its sweet and hot flavors and its "sunny" color. It is an inspired addition to cream cheese or to a wedge of Canadian Cheddar. While best with cheeses, it also goes well with warm biscuits and omelets.

6	peaches, peeled, pitted and chopped	6
6	sweet yellow peppers, seeded and chopped	6
1	hot yellow pepper, seeded and chopped	1
1	lemon, halved	1
½ cup	white wine vinegar	125 mL
2½ cups	granulated sugar	625 mL
1½ tsp	pickling salt	7 mL

1. Place peaches, peppers, lemon and vinegar in a large stainless steel or enamel saucepan. Bring to a boil over medium-high heat, reduce heat and boil gently, uncovered, for 30 minutes or until softened. Remove and discard lemon, add sugar and salt; return to a boil. Cook, uncovered, for about 20 minutes or until mixture thickens, stirring frequently.

2. Remove hot jars from canner and ladle relish into jars to within ½ inch (1 cm) of rim (headspace). Process 10 minutes for 1-cup (250 mL) jars and 15 minutes for 2-cup (500 mL) jars as directed on page 14 (Easy Step-by-Step Preserving).

Makes 4 cups (1 L).

Caramelized Red Onion Relish

Balsamic vinegar is the magic ingredient in this recipe. It adds a pungent sweetness to the caramelized onions. Serve with barbecued or broiled meats such as steak, lamb chops and chicken.

2	large red onions, peeled	2
¼ cup	firmly packed brown sugar	50 mL
1 cup	dry red wine	250 mL
3 tbsp	balsamic vinegar	45 mL
⅛ tsp	each: salt and freshly ground pepper	0.5 mL

1. Slice onions into very thin slices. Combine onions and sugar in a heavy non-stick skillet. Cook, uncovered, over medium-high heat for about 25 minutes or until onions turn golden and start to caramelize, stirring frequently.
2. Stir in wine and vinegar. Bring to a boil over high heat, reduce heat to low and cook for about 15 minutes or until most of the liquid has evaporated, stirring frequently.
3. Season to taste with salt and pepper. Spoon into a clean wide-mouthed jar and cool briefly.
4. Remove hot jars from canner and ladle relish into jars to within ½ inch (1 cm) of rim (headspace). Process 10 minutes for 1-cup (250 mL) jars as directed on page 14 (Easy Step-by-Step Preserving).

Makes 2 cups (500 mL).

Sweet Onion and Fennel Relish

Fennel's sweet, delicate hint of licorice is evident in this unique relish.

1	large sweet onion, such as Spanish or Vidalia (about 8 oz/250 g)	1
1	fennel bulb (about 10 oz/275 g)	1
1	sweet red pepper, seeded and sliced into thin strips	1
2½ tsp	pickling salt, divided	12 mL
1½ cups	white wine vinegar	375 mL
½ cup	water	125 mL
¼ cup	granulated sugar	50 mL
2	bay leaves	2
8	black peppercorns	8

1. Slice onion in half lengthwise, then in very thin slices crosswise to form half circles. Cut fennel bulb in half lengthwise and remove core; thinly slice crosswise to form half circles. Place onion, fennel and pepper in a non-reactive bowl and sprinkle with 2 tsp (10 mL) salt. Toss and let stand for 4 hours. Rinse twice and drain thoroughly.

2. Combine vinegar, water, sugar and ½ tsp (2 mL) salt in a large stainless steel or enamel saucepan. Bring to a boil over high heat. Add vegetables and return just to a boil, stirring constantly. Remove from heat.

3. Remove hot jars from canner. Remove vegetables from liquid with a slotted spoon and pack into jars. Pour liquid over vegetables to within ½ inch (1 cm) of rim (headspace). Add bay leaves and peppercorns.

4. Process 10 minutes for 1-cup (250 mL) jars and 15 minutes for 2-cup (500 mL) jars as directed on page 14 (Easy Step-by-Step Preserving).

Makes 4 cups (1 L).

Zucchini Garden Pepper Relish

Zucchini lends a lightness and freshness to traditional pepper relish.

4	medium zucchini (about 1¼ lb/625 g), finely chopped	4
2	medium onions, finely chopped	2
½	sweet red pepper, seeded and finely chopped	½
½	sweet green pepper, seeded and finely chopped	½
2 tbsp	pickling salt	25 mL
1¼ cups	granulated sugar	300 mL
¾ cup	cider vinegar	175 mL
1 tsp	each: dry mustard and celery seeds	5 mL
½ tsp	each: hot pepper flakes and turmeric	2 mL
1 tbsp	water	15 mL
2 tsp	cornstarch	10 mL

1. Toss together zucchini, onions and red and green peppers in a large non-reactive bowl. Sprinkle with salt and stir well. Let stand for 1 hour, stirring occasionally.
2. Drain vegetables in a sieve and rinse; drain again, pressing out excess moisture.
3. Combine drained vegetables, sugar, vinegar, mustard, celery seeds, hot pepper flakes and turmeric in large stainless steel or enamel saucepan. Bring to a boil over high heat, reduce heat and boil gently, uncovered, for 15 minutes or until vegetables are tender.
4. Blend water and cornstarch; stir into vegetables. Cook for 5 minutes or until liquid clears and thickens, stirring often.
5. Remove hot jars from canner and ladle relish into jars to within ½ inch (1 cm) of rim (headspace). Process 10 minutes for 1-cup (250 mL) jars and 15 minutes for 2-cup (500 mL) jars as directed on page 14 (Easy Step-by-Step Preserving).

Makes 4 cups (1 L).

Brinjal Pickle Relish

Ellie first tasted this relish in Australia and immediately set about finding a way to duplicate it. She found the secret of the relish's flavor in an old cookbook given to her by a visitor from Sri Lanka—sautéing the diced eggplant in "½ bottle of oil" before mixing it with "spiced pickle."

3 tbsp	vegetable oil	45 mL
1	eggplant, cut into ¼-inch (5mm) cubes	1
2–3	hot red chile peppers, seeded and finely chopped	2–3
3	large cloves garlic, finely chopped	3
¾ cup	white vinegar	175 mL
4 tsp	chili powder	20 mL
1 tbsp	whole fenugreek	15 mL
1 tsp	ground coriander	5 mL
½ tsp	dry mustard	2 mL
¼ tsp	each: turmeric and salt	1 mL
½ cup	brown sugar	125 mL

1. Heat oil over medium heat in a large nonstick skillet. Add eggplant and sauté gently for about 10 minutes. (At first the oil is completely absorbed, but then is gradually released as the eggplant becomes fairly firm). Stir in chile peppers and garlic; cook for 3 minutes.
2. Stir in vinegar, chili powder, fenugreek, coriander, mustard, turmeric and salt. Bring to a boil, reduce heat and boil gently for about 10 minutes. Add sugar and cook for 2 minutes.
3. Remove hot jars from canner and ladle relish into jars to within ½ inch (1 cm) of rim (headspace). Process 15 minutes for 1-cup (250 mL) jars and 20 minutes for 2-cup (500 mL) jars as directed on page 14 (Easy Step-by-Step Preserving).

Makes 2 cups (500 mL).

Indian-Style Cucumber Relish

Seasoned with traditional spices, cumin, and black and yellow mustard seeds, this relish shows its East Indian heritage. Use it to pep up meats or poultry. Mixed with yogurt it becomes raita, a salad that is served with Indian food as a cool counterpoint to spicy dishes.

6 cups	diced peeled cucumber	
	(about 8–12 medium pickling cucumbers)	1.5 L
2 cups	thinly sliced onions	500 mL
1 tbsp	pickling salt	15 mL
2 cups	white vinegar	500 mL
½ cup	granulated sugar	125 mL
1 tbsp	whole cumin seeds	15 mL
2 tsp	black mustard seeds	10 mL
2 tsp	yellow mustard seeds	10 mL

1. Place cucumber and onion in a non-reactive bowl and sprinkle with salt. Let stand for 4 hours, stirring occasionally. Drain vegetables in a sieve, rinse twice and drain thoroughly.
2. Combine vinegar, sugar, cumin seeds and mustard seeds in a very large stainless steel or enamel saucepan. Bring to a boil over high heat. Add vegetables and return to a boil for 30 seconds.
3. Remove hot jars from canner. Remove vegetables from liquid with a slotted spoon; pack into jars. Pour liquid over cucumber to within ½ inch (1 cm) of rim (headspace).
4. Process 10 minutes for 1-cup (250 mL) jars and 15 minutes for 2-cup (500 mL) jars as directed on page 14 (Easy Step-by-Step Preserving).

Makes 6 cups (1.5 L).

Cauliflower Chow Chow

Chow chow has come to refer to a relish of mixed vegetables in a mustard sauce.

3 cups	cauliflower florets, coarsely chopped (about ½ head)	750 mL
2	small pickling cucumbers, peeled and chopped	2
1	sweet green pepper, seeded and chopped	1
1	small hot red chile pepper, seeded peeled and chopped	1
1	onion, chopped	1
3 tbsp	pickling salt	45 mL
3 cups	lukewarm water	750 mL
⅔ cup	granulated sugar	150 mL
3 tbsp	all-purpose flour	45 mL
2 tsp	each: dry mustard and celery seeds	10 mL
½ tsp	each: curry powder and turmeric	2 mL
⅔ cup	each: cider vinegar and white vinegar	150 mL
⅓ cup	water	75 mL

1. Toss together cauliflower, cucumbers, green pepper, chile pepper and onion in a large non-reactive bowl. Stir salt and lukewarm water together and pour over vegetables. Let stand for 8 to 10 hours. Drain vegetables in a sieve; rinse twice and drain thoroughly.

2. Combine sugar, flour, mustard, celery seeds, curry powder and turmeric in a large stainless steel or enamel saucepan. Add vinegars and water, stirring to blend well. Bring to a boil over high heat, stirring constantly until mixture thickens. Add the drained vegetables, return to a boil, reduce heat and boil gently, uncovered, for 10 minutes.

3. Remove hot jars from canner and ladle relish into jars to within ½ inch (1 cm) of rim (headspace). Process 10 minutes for 1-cup (250 mL) jars and 15 minutes for 2-cup (500 mL) jars as directed on page 14 (Easy Step-by-Step Preserving).

Makes 3½ cups (875 mL).

Caponata

Caponata is a Sicilian dish served as a salad, side dish or relish.

1	small eggplant, cut into ¼-inch (5 mm) cubes	1
1½ tbsp	pickling salt	20 mL
2	large tomatoes, peeled and chopped	2
1	medium sweet red pepper, seeded and diced	1
1 cup	diced zucchini	250 mL
½ cup	chopped onion	125 mL
3	large cloves garlic, chopped	3
¼ cup	chopped stuffed olives	50 mL
1 tbsp	capers, rinsed	15 mL
1	bay leaf	1
1 tsp	fresh thyme or ¼ tsp (1 mL) dried	5 mL
¼ tsp	each: salt and freshly ground pepper	1 mL
⅓ cup	red wine vinegar	75 mL
2 tsp	each: granulated sugar and olive oil	10 mL
2 tbsp	tomato paste	25 mL

1. Place eggplant in a non-reactive bowl. Sprinkle with salt and stir well. Let stand for 2 hours. Drain eggplant in a sieve and rinse twice, draining thoroughly; press out excess moisture.
2. Place eggplant, tomatoes, red pepper, zucchini, onion, garlic, olives, capers, bay leaf, thyme, salt and pepper in a large roasting pan.
3. Heat vinegar, sugar and oil in a microwavable container until hot, about 1 minute; stir into vegetables. Bake in a 350°F (180°C) oven for about 1½ hours (1 hour for a convection oven), or until vegetables are softened and liquid has evaporated, stirring every 20 minutes. Remove pan from oven, discard bay leaf and stir in tomato paste.
4. Remove hot jars from canner and spoon relish into jars to within ½ inch (1 cm) of rim (headspace). Process 15 minutes for 1-cup (250 mL) jars and 20 minutes for 2-cup (500 mL) jars as directed on page 14 (Easy Step-by-Step Preserving).

Makes 5 cups (1.25 L).

chapter 8

SALSA

RARELY do we open a food magazine without finding a mention of salsa. Salsas, the name given to a Mexican sauce, are either cooked or fresh mixtures of fruits and vegetables. The more salsas we make, the better we like them. Spicy or mild, chunky or smooth, and in colors of gold, green or red, salsas transform an otherwise plain meal into a dinner to remember.

Chile peppers of one type or another are usually added to salsa for flavor and to give authenticity. Some chiles can be positively fiery while others are quite mild. Just how mouth-searing a chile is depends on the amount of capsaicin, an acidic chemical, concentrated in the veins and seeds. That's why removing veins and seeds lower the heat level. As a rule of thumb, the smaller and more pointed the chile, the hotter it is. Remember to always wear rubber gloves when handling all hot chile peppers and never touch your mouth or eyes. Chile peppers are interchangeable in most recipes, so experiment with their differing flavors and heat levels. See the Chile Pepper Heat Scale on the following page.

Tomatillos are another Mexican specialty. We love to make our Tomatillo Mexican Salsa (page 194) whenever they are available. Fresh coriander also gives an authentic Mexican flavor to salsa. It is easily found today in supermarkets, sometimes referred to as Chinese parsley, other times as fresh cilantro.

Fresh uncooked salsas should be kept refrigerated and consumed quickly, as you would with any other fresh food. Most salsas are made from assorted vegetables. But fruit salsas are gaining popularity, so we have added several including Fresh Pineapple Jalapeño Salsa (page 207) and Papaya Mango Salsa (page 197).

Serving Suggestions:

Salsas really jazz up plain old ground beef, whether in a meat loaf or in patties. Fajitas, enchiladas and Tacos wouldn't be the same without salsa. Add some salsa to low-fat sour cream or plain yogurt to make a light dip. Be adventurous and mix salsa with pasta for a speedy supper. And perhaps the best way to eat salsa is alone with your favorite dippers!

Chile Pepper Heat Scale

Rating	Varieties
10 (hottest)	Habanero, Scotch Bonnet
9	Santaka, Chiltepin, Thai
8	Aji, Rocoto, Piquin, Cayenne, Tabasco
7	de Arbol
6	Yellow Hot Wax, Serrano
5	Jalapeño, Mirasol
4	Sandia, Cascabel
3	Ancho, Pasilla, Espanola
2	NuMex Big Jim
1	Mexi-Bell, Cherry
0	Sweet Bell, Pimiento, Sweet Banana

List of Recipes: Salsas

Your Basic Chunky Tomato Salsa

Make this basic salsa in the fall when ingredients are at their freshest.
We believe its many variations will suit your family's preferences.

8	medium tomatoes, peeled and chopped (about 2 lb/1 kg)	8
2	medium onions, finely chopped	2
1	sweet green pepper, seeded and chopped	1
2–6	jalapeño peppers, halved, seeded and chopped	2–6
6	cloves garlic, minced	6
1 cup	tomato sauce	250 mL
1 cup	red wine vinegar	250 mL
1 cup	chopped fresh parsley	250 mL
1 tbsp	granulated sugar	15 mL
1 tsp	pickling salt	5 mL
1 tsp	ground cumin	5 mL

1. Combine tomatoes, onion, green pepper, jalapeño peppers, garlic, tomato sauce, vinegar, parsley, sugar, salt and cumin in a medium stainless steel or enamel saucepan. Bring to a boil over high heat, reduce heat and boil gently, uncovered, for 25 minutes or until desired consistency, stirring frequently.

2. Remove hot jars from canner and ladle salsa into jars to within ½ inch (1 cm) of rim (headspace). Process 20 minutes for 1-cup (250 mL) and 2-cup (500 mL) jars as directed on page 14 (Easy Step-by-Step Preserving).

Makes 5 cups (1.25 L).

Beyond Hot Salsa

Commonly known as piquant, this salsa is not for the timid. If it's too piquant for your taste, cut the heat by reducing the amount of red hot chile peppers. If it's not piquant enough, be our guest and replace some of the jalapeño peppers with more hot chiles.

8	plum tomatoes (about 2 lb/1 kg)	8
1	large onion	1
4	large cloves garlic	4
4–5	jalapeño peppers, seeded (*see Tip*)	4–5
2	small hot red chile peppers, seeded	2
¼ cup	cider vinegar	50 mL
2 tsp	dried oregano leaves or 2 tbsp (25 mL) chopped fresh	10 mL
1 tsp	each: pickling salt and granulated sugar	5 mL

1. Combine tomatoes, onion, garlic and peppers in a food processor or blender; process until smooth. Transfer to a medium stainless steel or enamel saucepan.
2. Add vinegar, oregano, salt and sugar. Bring to a boil over high heat, reduce heat and boil gently, uncovered, for about 15 minutes or until the salsa is thickened.
3. Remove hot jars from canner and ladle salsa into jars to within ½ inch (1 cm) of top rim (headspace). Process 20 minutes for 1-cup (250 mL) and 2-cup (500 mL) jars as directed on page 14 (Easy Step-by-Step Preserving).

Makes 3 cups (750 mL).

tip | *Jalapeño peppers vary in heat level from hot to very hot, but you cannot tell the heat level from their appearance.*

Fiery Yellow Pepper Salsa

This salsa has lots of heat. If you don't like your salsa this hot, use more sweet pepper in place of the hot ones. Just don't change the total amount of peppers. Remember that the heat of individual peppers can vary greatly. This salsa is a peppery dip for nacho chips or a bold accompaniment to grilled chicken, beef or pork.

2 cups	chopped sweet yellow pepper	500 mL
2 cups	chopped peeled ripe tomatoes (about 2 medium tomatoes)	500 mL
½ cup	finely chopped red onion	125 mL
¼ cup	finely chopped hot yellow pepper	50 mL
¼ cup	finely chopped jalapeño pepper	50 mL
2	large cloves garlic, minced	2
¼ cup	lime juice	50 mL
2 tbsp	white vinegar	25 mL
½ tsp	pickling salt	2 mL
2 tbsp	finely chopped fresh coriander	25 mL

1. Combine sweet pepper, tomatoes, onion, hot peppers, garlic, lime juice, vinegar and salt in a medium stainless steel or enamel saucepan. Bring to a boil over high heat, reduce heat and boil gently, uncovered, for about 15 minutes or until mixture is thickened, stirring frequently. Stir in coriander and cook for 2 minutes.
2. Remove hot jars from canner and ladle salsa into jars to within ½ inch (1 cm) of rim (headspace). Process 20 minutes for 1-cup (250 mL) and 2-cup (500 mL) jars as directed on page 14 (Easy Step-by-Step Preserving).

Makes 3 cups (750 mL).

Garden Patch Salsa

This mixed vegetable salsa is an excellent accompaniment to burgers and cheese nachos or as a low-fat topping for a baked potato. Try it as a zesty dip.

6	tomatoes, peeled and diced (1½ lb/750 g)	6
4	jalapeño peppers, seeded and minced	4
2	cloves garlic, minced	2
1 cup	chopped onion	250 mL
1 cup	each: shredded carrot and shredded zucchini	250 mL
½ cup	each: chopped sweet green pepper and chopped sweet yellow pepper	125 mL
½ cup	chopped Italian (flat-leaf) parsley	125 mL
½ cup	white vinegar	125 mL
⅓ cup	tomato paste	75 mL
¼ cup	chopped fresh oregano or 1 tbsp (15 mL) dried	50 mL
½ tsp	pickling salt	2 mL

1. Place all ingredients in a large stainless steel or enamel saucepan. Bring to a boil over high heat, reduce heat and simmer, uncovered, for 30 minutes or until thickened.
2. Remove hot jars from canner and ladle salsa into jars to within ½ inch (1 cm) of rim (headspace). Process 20 minutes for 1-cup (250 mL) and 2-cup (500 mL) jars as directed on page 14 (Easy Step-by-Step Preserving).

Makes 5½ cups (1.375 L).

Gazpacho Salsa

Gazpacho, that great Spanish cold soup from Andalucia, always makes us think of summertime. So does this salsa. However, this salsa can be made anytime but the flavors are always at their best in summer, when garden-ripened produce is used.

1 tbsp	olive oil	15 mL
½ cup	finely chopped onion	125 mL
2	cloves garlic, minced	2
4	large tomatoes, peeled and chopped (about 3 cups/750 mL)	4
½ cup	diced peeled seedless cucumber	125 mL
½ cup	diced sweet green pepper	125 mL
2 cups	tomato juice	500 mL
⅓ cup	red wine vinegar	75 mL
1 tbsp	Worcestershire sauce	15 mL
1 tsp	each: ground cumin and paprika	5 mL
2 tbsp	chopped fresh basil	25 mL
	salt and freshly ground pepper, to taste	

1. Heat oil in a large stainless steel or enamel saucepan and sauté onion on medium heat for 5 minutes. Add garlic and cook for 1 minute.
2. Stir in tomatoes, cucumber, green pepper, tomato juice, vinegar, Worcestershire sauce, cumin and paprika. Bring to a boil over high heat, reduce heat and boil gently, uncovered, for about 30 minutes or until mixture is thickened, stirring occasionally. Stir in basil, salt and pepper and cook for 2 minutes.
3. Remove hot jars from canner and ladle salsa into jars to within ½ inch (1 cm) of rim (headspace). Process 20 minutes for 1-cup (250 mL) and 2-cup (500 mL) jars as directed on page 14 (Easy Step-by-Step Preserving).

Makes 4 cups (1 L).

Tomatillo Mexican Salsa

Tomatillos are finding favor with salsa lovers for their fresh tart flavor and hint of lemon and apple. Choose tomatillos that have their husks intact and are still green. They may be kept in a paper bag in the refrigerator for up to a month. If you can't find tomatillos, green tomatoes may be substituted. Choose pale green rather than dark green tomatoes to avoid solanine, a potentially toxic substance that disappears as the tomato ripens.

½ lb	tomatillos (about 7 tomatillos)	250 g
2	hot green chile peppers, seeded and chopped	2
2	cloves garlic, minced	2
½ cup	chopped sweet red pepper	125 mL
½ cup	chopped onion	125 mL
½ cup	chopped carrot	125 mL
¼ cup	each: apple juice and cider vinegar	50 mL
¾ tsp	pickling salt	4 mL
½ tsp	each: ground cumin and dried oregano	2 mL
1 tbsp	granulated sugar	15 mL

1. Remove husks from tomatillos and discard. Wash tomatillos and coarsely chop in a food processor or by hand. Transfer to a medium stainless steel or enamel saucepan; add chiles, garlic, red pepper, onion, carrot, apple juice, vinegar, salt, cumin and oregano. Bring to a boil over high heat, reduce heat, cover and boil gently for 10 minutes.
2. Stir in sugar, return to a boil and boil gently, uncovered, for 20 minutes or until mixture is thickened. Remove from heat.
3. Remove hot jars from canner and ladle salsa into jars to within ½ inch (1 cm) of rim (headspace). Process 20 minutes for 1-cup (250 mL) jars as directed on page 14 (Easy Step-by-Step Preserving).

Makes 2 cups (500 mL).

Southwest Salsa

Here is another basic recipe for salsa. The original asked for the juice of a Seville orange. Since these bitter oranges are not always available, we substituted a blend of lime and sweet orange juice. The salsa is best made when field-ripened tomatoes are in season. Make enough to last till they are available again!

4 cups	chopped peeled tomatoes (about 2 lb/1 kg)	1 L
1 cup	chopped onion	250 mL
3	cloves garlic, minced	3
½ cup	chopped sweet red pepper	125 mL
2–4	jalapeño peppers, seeded and minced	2–4
½ cup	red wine vinegar	125 mL
¼ cup	chopped fresh coriander	50 mL
2 tbsp	orange juice	25 mL
1 tbsp	lime juice	15 mL
1 tsp	each: granulated sugar and pickling salt	5 mL
¼ cup	tomato paste	50 mL

1. Combine tomatoes, onion, garlic, peppers, vinegar, coriander, orange and lime juice, sugar and salt in a large stainless steel or enamel saucepan. Bring to a boil over high heat, reduce heat and boil gently, uncovered, for 30 minutes or until mixture is thickened, stirring occasionally. Stir in tomato paste and cook for 2 minutes.
2. Remove hot jars from canner and ladle salsa into jars to within ½ inch (1 cm) of rim (headspace). Process 20 minutes for 1-cup (250 mL) and 2-cup (500 mL) jars as directed on page 14 (Easy Step-by-Step Preserving).

Makes 4 cups (1 L).

Salsa Bruschetta-Style

Bruschetta has its origins in ancient Rome. During the December and January holidays, Romans celebrated by eating flat buns soaked in olive oil still fresh from the fall harvest. The name bruschetta comes from the Italian bruscare, meaning "to roast over coals." This topping is a favorite of ours to have on hand for making a quick appetizer.

3 cups	chopped peeled Italian plum tomatoes	
	(1½ lb/750 g)	750 mL
2	large cloves garlic, minced	2
2	shallots, minced	2
1 cup	chopped fresh basil	250 mL
1 tbsp	red wine vinegar	15 mL
1 tsp	lemon juice	5 mL
½ tsp	pickling salt	2 mL
¼ tsp	coarsely ground black pepper	1 mL
2	green onions, minced	2
3 tbsp	tomato paste	45 mL

1. Combine tomatoes, garlic, shallots, basil, vinegar, lemon juice, salt and pepper in a medium stainless steel or enamel saucepan. Bring to a boil over high heat, reduce heat and boil gently for 5 minutes, stirring frequently. Stir in green onion, tomato paste and return to a boil.
2. Remove hot jars from canner and ladle salsa into jars to within ½ inch (1 cm) of rim (headspace). Process 20 minutes for 1-cup (250 mL) and 2-cup (500 mL) jars as directed on page 14 (Easy Step-by-Step Preserving).

Makes 3 cups (750 mL).

Papaya Mango Salsa

This is a true fruit salsa and it's processed to keep on the shelf. Its papaya, mango and pineapple flavors go particularly well with fish.

1	papaya, peeled, seeded and chopped	1
1	mango, peeled and chopped	1
1	jalapeño pepper, seeded and finely chopped	1
	juice and grated rind of 1 lime	
¼ cup	unsweetened pineapple juice	50 mL
1 tbsp	finely chopped Candied Ginger	
	or crystallized ginger	15 mL
1 tbsp	rice wine vinegar	15 mL
¼ tsp	pickling salt	1 mL
2 tbsp	chopped fresh mint	25 mL

1. Place papaya, mango, jalapeño pepper, lime juice and rind, pineapple juice, ginger, vinegar and salt in a medium saucepan. Bring to a boil over high heat, reduce heat and boil gently for 1 minute. Stir in mint, return to a boil and cook for 1 minute.
2. Remove hot jars from canner and ladle salsa into jars to within ½ inch (1 cm) of rim (headspace). Process 20 minutes for 1-cup (250 mL) jars as directed on page 14 (Easy Step-by-Step Preserving).

Makes 2 cups (500 mL).

Peach Mint Salsa

The sunny taste of peaches and the cool freshness of mint combine in this lovely fruit salsa to say "summer." Make this quick salsa when peaches are at their flavor peak. Its fresh taste beautifully complements grilled chicken and fish.

2 cups	chopped peeled peaches	
	(about 4 medium peaches)	500 mL
¼ cup	finely chopped red onion	50 mL
¼ cup	finely chopped sweet green pepper	50 mL
1 tbsp	finely chopped jalapeño pepper	15 mL
2 tbsp	liquid honey	25 mL
¼ tsp	pickling salt	1 mL
	grated rind and juice of 1 lime	
2 tbsp	finely chopped fresh mint	25 mL

1. Combine peaches, onion, peppers, honey, salt, lime rind and juice in a medium stainless steel or enamel saucepan. Bring to a boil over high heat, reduce heat and boil gently, uncovered, for 5 minutes, stirring occasionally.
2. Stir in mint and cook for 1 minute.
3. Remove hot jars from canner and ladle salsa into jars to within ½ inch (1 cm) of rim (headspace). Process 20 minutes for 1-cup (250 mL) jars as directed on page 14 (Easy Step-by-Step Preserving).

Makes 2 cups (500 mL).

Fresh and Dried Cranberry Salsa

Dried cranberries are added to fresh or frozen ones in this salsa to create a more concentrated cranberry flavor. They are then cooked with the rest of the ingredients to bring out their best flavor. Use this salsa as an alternative to cranberry sauce or jelly.

1 cup	fresh or frozen cranberries, coarsely chopped	250 mL
¼ cup	dried cranberries	50 mL
¼ cup	chopped red onion	50 mL
2 tbsp	chopped fresh parsley	25 mL
1–2 tbsp	liquid honey	15–25 mL
1 tbsp	each: red wine vinegar and lemon juice	15 mL
2 tsp	granulated sugar	10 mL
¼ tsp	each: pickling salt and hot pepper flakes	1 mL

1. Combine cranberries, onion, parsley, honey, vinegar, lemon juice, sugar, salt and pepper flakes in a medium stainless steel or enamel saucepan. Bring to a boil over medium heat, reduce heat and boil gently, uncovered, for about 10 minutes or until mixture is thickened, stirring frequently.
2. Remove hot jars from canner and ladle salsa into jars to within ½ inch (1 cm) of rim (headspace). Process 20 minutes for 1-cup (250 mL) jars as directed on page 14 (Easy Step-by-Step Preserving).

Makes 1¼ cups (300 mL).

Fresh Vegetable Salsas

Salsas originated in Mexico, where they are always served fresh and so are best eaten immediately or at the most in a day or two. Fresh tomato salsas are by far the most common, but more and more ingredients, particularly fruits and other vegetables, are finding their way into this popular condiment.

Vegetable salsas are the everyday salsas of the salsa-eating world. Made and used fresh, or refrigerated for a short time, these salsas do not require as much vinegar as those that are processed and stored for later use.

Pico de Gallo Salsa

Pico de Gallo is a blend of hot chile peppers and other fresh vegetables. Variations of this salsa can be found on every Mexican restaurant table to eat with crisp corn or flour tortillas. It is excellent as a dip, and also as a salsa on tacos and enchiladas and with grilled meats and poultry. We hope it will become as popular in your home as in ours.

4	plum tomatoes, chopped (about 2 cups/500 mL)	4
½ cup	chopped red onion	125 mL
½ cup	chopped cucumber	125 mL
1	large clove garlic, minced	1
1	small jalapeño pepper, seeded and minced	1
¼ cup	chopped fresh coriander	50 mL
¼ cup	lime juice	50 mL

1. Combine tomatoes, onion, cucumber, garlic, jalapeño pepper, coriander and lime juice. Stir well.
2. Cover and refrigerate for 30 minutes (longer is unnecessary as this salsa is best when freshly made).

Makes about 3 cups (750 mL).

Fresh Tomato and Black Olive Salsa

The olives convert this basic Mexican dish to something more Spanish or maybe Italian. It's good as an appetizer with crackers or squares of toasted Italian bread and is best served at room temperature.

2 cups	diced plum tomatoes (about 4)	500 mL
½ cup	chopped pitted black olives(preferably Kalamata)	125 mL
⅓ cup	chopped red onion	75 mL
2 tbsp	red wine vinegar	25 mL
1	clove garlic, minced	1
1 tbsp	Dijon mustard	15 mL
	freshly ground black pepper	

1. Combine tomatoes, olives, onion, vinegar, garlic, mustard and pepper to taste. Stir well.
2. Cover and let stand at room temperature for a few hours. Or place in tightly sealed containers and refrigerate up to 2 weeks.

Makes about 2½ cups (625 mL).

Garlic Tomato Salsa

An easy-to-make fresh salsa chock full of flavor. Even non-garlic lovers may become addicted.

2	ripe medium tomatoes, chopped	2
2	cloves garlic, crushed	2
2 tbsp	lime juice	25 mL
1 tbsp	chopped fresh coriander or parsley	15 mL
1 tbsp	finely chopped red onion	15 mL
1 tsp	capers, drained and chopped	5 mL
⅛ tsp	salt	0.5 mL

Combine tomatoes, garlic, lime juice, coriander, onion, capers and salt in a small bowl. Cover and let stand in refrigerator for 15 minutes.

Makes 1 cup (250 mL).

Triple Tomato Salsa

Three kinds of tomatoes—cherry, tomatillo and common—are the basis of this appealing salsa. It has become one of our favorite dips for tortilla chips. If you can find orange or yellow cherry tomatoes, they add interesting color.

1 tbsp	extra virgin olive oil	15 mL
½ cup	chopped red onion	125 mL
2 tbsp	dry white wine	25 mL
8	green tomatillos, husked, cored and diced (see Tip)	8
4	ripe medium tomatoes, seeded and diced	4
2 cups	yellow, orange or red cherry tomatoes, diced salt and freshly ground pepper	500 mL
6	sprigs fresh basil, chopped	6

1. Heat oil in a large non-stick skillet over medium-high heat. Add onion and cook for 2 minutes. Add wine and tomatillos; stir to combine. Remove from heat.
2. Add tomatoes to skillet while it is still warm. Season to taste with salt and pepper; stir in basil.
3. Place mixture in a medium bowl. Cover and let stand for 20 minutes. Refrigerate until serving time, but use within 6 hours.

Makes 3 cups (750 mL).

tip | *If you are unable to buy tomatillos, replace with diced pale green tomatoes.*

Roasted Corn and Sweet Pepper Salsa

Roasting sweet corn caramelizes the sugar in the kernels into a wonderful woodsy flavor that is highlighted by balsamic vinegar and sweet peppers.

1½ cups	fresh corn kernels (about 3 ears)	375 mL
1 tsp	olive oil	5 mL
¼ cup	each: diced sweet orange pepper and sweet green pepper	50 mL
¼ cup	diced red onion	50 mL
2 tbsp	chopped fresh Italian parsley	25 mL
2 tsp	each: balsamic vinegar and lime juice	10 mL
⅛ tsp	salt	0.5 mL

1. Heat a large non-stick skillet over medium-high heat. Add corn and oil and cook until corn turns a light brown, stirring constantly.
2. Remove from heat and cool for 5 minutes.
3. Stir in peppers, onion, parsley, vinegar, lime juice and salt.
4. Cover and let stand for 30 minutes before serving.

Makes 1½ cups (375 mL).

Tapenade-Style Salsa

This salsa has a more paste-like consistency than most and with its olive and garlic flavors reminds us of the French tapenade. It is marvelous spread on sliced crusty Italian bread or on crackers.

¾ cup	chopped pitted Kalamata olives	175 mL
⅔ cup	chopped pitted green olives	150 mL
½	sweet red pepper, seeded and chopped	½ cup
	chopped sun-dried tomatoes in olive oil	50 mL
¼ cup	chopped Italian (flat-leaf) parsley	50 mL
¼ cup	olive oil	50 mL
2	cloves garlic, chopped	2
1 tbsp	each: red wine vinegar and balsamic vinegar	15 mL
	freshly ground black pepper	

1. Place olives, red pepper, dried tomatoes, parsley, oil, garlic, red wine vinegar and balsamic vinegar in a food processor and process with on/off motion until finely chopped. Add black pepper to taste.
2. Spoon salsa into clean jars or plastic containers to within ½ inch (1 cm) of rim. Cover with tight-fitting lids.
3. Label jars and refrigerate for up to 1 week or freeze for longer storage.

Makes 2 cups (500 mL).

Fresh Fruit Salsas

Although vegetable salsas are by far the most common, trendy fresh
fruit salsas are appearing more frequently. Their uses are many—and
everyone eats large amounts as a side dish, so make lots. They are
refreshing.

Fresh Spicy Tropical Fruit Salsa

Tropical flavors abound in this fresh fruit salsa. We found that its fresh
and minty flavors beautifully complement grilled sausages, pork chops,
pork tenderloin and chicken.

1	kiwifruit, peeled and diced	1
¼	mango, peeled and diced	¼
¼	papaya, peeled, seeded and chopped	¼
½ cup	quartered strawberries	125 mL
½ cup	diced cantaloupe	125 mL
½	jalapeño or other hot pepper, seeded and finely chopped	½
2 tbsp	finely chopped fresh mint	25 mL
1 tbsp	each: granulated sugar and lime juice	15 mL

1. Gently stir together kiwifruit, mango, papaya, strawberries, canta-
   loupe and jalapeño.
2. Add mint, sugar and lime juice; stir to blend.
3. Refrigerate for about 10 minutes to allow flavors to develop.

Makes 3 cups (750 mL).

Fresh Sweet Pepper and Peach Salsa

Peaches are to summer as apples are to fall, and this salsa is certainly a celebration of the summer peach season.

4 cups	chopped peeled peaches (4 medium)	1 L
½	small sweet red pepper, seeded and chopped	½
½	small sweet green pepper, seeded and chopped	½
¼ cup	finely chopped red onion	50 mL
¼ cup	chopped fresh coriander	50 mL
1 tbsp	chopped jalapeño or other hot pepper	15 mL
1	clove garlic, crushed	1
1 tbsp	each: lime juice and rice vinegar	15 mL
1 tsp	liquid honey	5 mL

Combine peaches, sweet peppers, onion, coriander, jalapeño pepper and garlic in a medium bowl. Stir in lime juice, vinegar and honey. Cover and refrigerate for 30 minutes for flavors to develop.

Makes about 3½ cups (875 mL).

Mango Coriander Salsa

Make this salsa whenever fresh mangoes are plentiful and inexpensive, usually from mid June till the end of July.

1	ripe medium mango	1
3 tbsp	chopped fresh coriander	45 mL
2	green onions, thinly sliced	2
1–2 tbsp	finely chopped jalapeño pepper	15–25 mL
1 tsp	lime juice	5 mL
½ tsp	granulated sugar	2 mL
⅛ tsp	each: salt and ground ginger	0.5 mL

Peel and dice mango into small pieces. Combine mango, coriander, onions, jalapeño pepper, lime juice, sugar, salt and ginger in a small bowl. Adjust seasonings, if desired. Serve immediately or cover and refrigerate for up to 1 day.

Makes about 1¼ cups (300 mL).

Fresh Pineapple Jalapeño Salsa

Hot jalapeño pepper and sweet, cooling pineapple blend to produce a salsa to serve with grilled chicken or fish. We did, and everyone wanted the recipe.

3	plum tomatoes, diced	3
1 cup	diced fresh pineapple	250 mL
1 cup	diced papaya	250 mL
¼ cup	chopped fresh coriander	50 mL
2	green onions, chopped	2
2	small jalapeño peppers, seeded and finely chopped	2
2 tbsp	lime juice	25 mL
⅛ tsp	each: salt and freshly ground pepper	0.5 mL

1. Combine tomatoes, pineapple, papaya, coriander, onions and jalapeño in a bowl.
2. Stir in lime juice, salt and pepper. Cover and refrigerate for 3 hours before serving. Stir again and transfer to a serving bowl.

Makes 2½ cups (625 mL).

Paradise Papaya Salsa

Colorful as well as flavorful, this salsa goes well with fruit salads, cottage cheese and chicken.

2 cups	diced peeled papaya	500 mL
½ cup	chopped sweet red pepper	125 mL
2	green onions, chopped	2
4 tsp	lime juice	20 mL
2 tsp	balsamic vinegar	10 mL
1	clove garlic, minced	1
	salt and freshly ground pepper	

Combine papaya, red pepper, onions, lime juice, vinegar and garlic. Cover and let stand for about 1 hour. Add salt and pepper to taste.

Makes 2½ cups (625 mL).

Tri-Color Citrus Mint Salsa

Multi-hued citrus gives a pleasing appearance as well as a refreshing flavor to this delightful salsa. It is particularly good with fish and chicken entrées.

2	medium pink grapefruit	2
2	large oranges	2
2	limes	2
1	jalapeño pepper, seeded and minced	1
2 tsp	finely minced shallots	10 mL
1 tsp	liquid honey	5 mL
⅛ tsp	salt	0.5 mL
3–4 drops	hot pepper sauce	3–4 drops

1. Remove outside rind from grapefruit, oranges and limes with a sharp knife, exposing the pulp of the fruit. Carefully cut on both sides of each inner membrane and gently lift out fruit sections. Cut each section into several pieces and place in a bowl. Drain off extra juice and reserve for another use.
2. Stir in pepper, shallots, honey, salt and hot pepper sauce. Refrigerate for about an hour to allow flavors to blend. Salsa may be prepared up to 1 day ahead.

Makes 2 cups (500 mL).

Tomato and chili sauce

Mustards

Orange marmalade

Microwave Lemon Curd

chapter 9

CHUTNEY

CHUTNEYS offer a whole new dimension to foods. Whereas salsas have a light and fresh, lively taste, chutneys have a rich, smooth, mellow, sweet-sour taste. They are a perfect accompaniment to spicy and strong-flavored foods. Like salsas, chutneys can range in texture from chunky to smooth and in spiciness from mild to hot.

Traditionally, apples and onions are the base of chutney ingredients, with raisins and sometimes dates added. Since dried fruits are often a main ingredient, many chutneys can be made at any time of the year. Chopping can be done with a food processor because all the ingredients become very soft during the cooking. Long, slow cooking is the general rule in making chutneys in order to develop their mellow flavor. Chutneys get better with age, so allow a few weeks in the jar after processing.

Mango Chutney (page 218) is probably the best known of all the chutneys. The addition of papaya in our Mango Papaya Chutney (page 219) is a new approach to this all-time favorite. Hellfire Chutney (page 227), a unique chutney made from dried dates, is probably our most authentic recipe since it was brought with a family moving to Canada from India where chutneys were first created. Juniper Berry Chutney (page 217) has Scottish origins.

Serving Suggestions:

Chutneys are traditionally served as an accompaniment to hot meals like curries, rice dishes, stews and casseroles. But don't hesitate to pair them with roast chicken, lamb, beef, pork and game. Some chutneys greatly enhance fish. You can offer a selection of chutneys with barbecued meats as well as with salads and cold meats. We often serve them with such cheeses as Stilton, Brie, Camembert and Gorgonzola. Be sure to try them with a cottage cheese salad and the sweeter ones make delicious bread and cracker spreads. One day, a small amount of chutney remained in the bottom of a jar when a dip was needed. We stirred in an equal amount of plain low-fat yogurt and *voilà*—the chutney became a delicious dip for raw veggies!

List of Recipes: Chutneys

Apple Plum Chutney

Autumn flavors of apples, blue plums and tomatoes shine in this traditionally spiced chutney.

5 cups	chopped peeled and cored apples (about 5 medium apples)	1.25 L
2½ cups	chopped peeled tomatoes (about 3 large tomatoes)	625 mL
2 cups	chopped pitted blue plums (about 8–10 plums)	500 mL
2 cups	sultana raisins	500 mL
2 cups	cider vinegar	500 mL
⅔ cup	chopped onion	150 mL
2	cloves garlic, minced	2
2½ cups	demerara or lightly packed dark brown sugar	625 mL
2 tsp	curry powder	10 mL
¼ tsp	ground allspice	1 mL
¼ tsp	pickling salt	1 mL
⅛ tsp	cayenne	0.5 mL

1. Combine apples, tomatoes, plums, raisins, vinegar, onion and garlic in a very large stainless steel or enamel saucepan. Bring to a boil over high heat, reduce heat and boil gently, uncovered, for 30 minutes.
2. Add sugar, return to a boil and boil gently for 30 minutes or until thickened, stirring occasionally. Add curry powder, allspice, salt and cayenne; cook for 5 minutes, stirring frequently.
3. Remove hot jars from canner and ladle chutney into jars to within ½ inch (1 cm) of rim (headspace). Process 10 minutes for 1-cup (250 mL) jars and 15 minutes for 2-cup (500 mL) jars as directed on page 14 (Easy Step-by-Step Preserving).

Makes about 6 cups (1.5 L).

Quick Apple Cranberry Chutney

This colorful recipe is a breeze! Cooking time is particularly short
because of the high pectin content of both fruits. It's wonderfully spicy
with lamb, chicken, pork and game.

2 cups	chopped cranberries	500 mL
1 cup	finely chopped apple	250 mL
½ cup	each: finely chopped red onion and sweet red pepper	125 mL
½ cup	cider vinegar	125 mL
2	cloves garlic, minced	2
1 tbsp	finely chopped gingerroot	15 mL
½ cup	packed brown sugar	125 mL
¼ tsp	each: cumin and salt	1 mL
⅛ tsp	each: freshly ground pepper and hot pepper flakes	0.5 mL

1. Combine cranberries, apple, onion, red pepper, vinegar, garlic and
   gingerroot in a medium stainless steel or enamel saucepan. Bring
   to a boil over high heat, reduce heat and boil gently, covered, for
   5 minutes or until cranberries pop.
2. Add sugar, cumin, salt, pepper and hot pepper flakes. Cook for
   5 minutes or until thickened.
3. Remove hot jars from canner and ladle chutney into jars to within
   ½ inch (1 cm) of rim (headspace). Process 10 minutes for 1-cup
   (250 mL) jars as directed on page 14 (Easy Step-by-Step Preserving).

Makes 2 cups (500 mL).

Spiced Kiwifruit Apple Chutney

We enjoy making this chutney when few other fresh fruits are available. Try it as an appetizer with cream cheese. Its delicate flavor pairs well with fish.

7	kiwifruit, peeled and chopped (about 3 cups/750 mL)	7
2	apples, peeled, cored and chopped	2
¾ cup	finely chopped onion	175 mL
¾ cup	granulated sugar	175 mL
¾ cup	cider vinegar	175 mL
¼ cup	brown sugar	50 mL
⅓ cup	golden raisins	75 mL
2	cloves garlic, crushed	2
1 tsp	minced peeled gingerroot	5 mL
½ tsp	each: cinnamon and mustard seeds	2 mL
¼ tsp	each: cayenne pepper, ground cloves, nutmeg and salt	1 mL

1. Combine kiwifruit, apples, onion, granulated sugar, vinegar, brown sugar, raisins, garlic and gingerroot in a large stainless steel or enamel saucepan. Bring to a boil over high heat, reduce heat and boil gently, uncovered, for 25 minutes or until thickened and fruit is tender, stirring occasionally. Add cinnamon, mustard seeds, cayenne, cloves, nutmeg and salt; boil gently for a few minutes longer.

2. Remove hot jars from canner and ladle chutney into jars to within ½ inch (1 cm) of rim (headspace). Process 10 minutes for 1-cup (250 mL) jars and 15 minutes for 2-cup (500 mL) jars as directed on page 14 (Easy Step-by-Step Preserving).

Makes 4 cups (1 L).

Cherry Currant Chutney

Rich and thick, this exciting combination of cherries, currants and peppers makes an exquisite accompaniment to duck, roasted turkey and chicken, and even to sausages.

1	medium orange	1
3 cups	fresh or frozen chopped cherries	750 mL
¾ cup	finely chopped onion	175 mL
½	finely chopped sweet green pepper	½
½	finely chopped sweet red pepper	½
⅓ cup	dried currants	75 mL
½ cup	lightly packed brown sugar	125 mL
¼ cup	balsamic vinegar	50 mL
1	1-inch (2.5 cm) piece gingerroot, peeled and chopped	1
¼–½ tsp	dried red pepper flakes	1–2 mL
½ tsp	each: ground cardamom and salt	2 mL
¼ tsp	ground allspice	1 mL

1. Remove 3 thin strips, about 2 inches (5 cm) long, of outer rind from orange and finely chop; reserve orange pulp for another use. Combine rind, cherries, onion, peppers, currants, sugar, vinegar, gingerroot and seasonings in a medium stainless steel or enamel saucepan. Bring to a boil, reduce heat and boil gently, covered, for 20 minutes. Uncover and continue to boil gently for 30 minutes or until thickened, stirring frequently.
2. Remove hot jars from canner and ladle chutney into jars to within ½ inch (1 cm) of rim (headspace). Process 10 minutes for 1-cup (250 mL) jars as directed on page 14 (Easy Step-by-Step Preserving).

Makes about 2 cups (500 mL).

Indian Chutney

Along the lines of the commercial chutney known as Major Gray, this recipe has a somewhat zippier flavor than some of our others. We love it with curries and also as a light appetizer combined with low-fat sour cream or plain yogurt served with crackers or raw vegetables.

1 cup	chopped onion	250 mL
¾ cup	raisins	175 mL
¾ cup	cider vinegar	175 mL
1	medium orange, peeled and chopped	1
1	medium lemon, peeled and chopped	1
1	lime, peeled and chopped	1
¼ cup	each: lightly packed brown sugar and molasses	50 mL
¼ cup	finely chopped gingerroot	50 mL
4	cloves garlic, crushed	4
1 tbsp	mustard seeds	15 mL
½ tsp	each: hot pepper flakes and cinnamon	2 mL
¼ tsp	each: ground cloves and allspice	1 mL
⅛ tsp	cayenne pepper	0.5 mL

1. Combine onion, raisins, vinegar, orange, lemon, lime, brown sugar, molasses, gingerroot, garlic and mustard seeds in a large stainless steel or enamel saucepan. Bring to a boil over high heat, reduce heat and boil gently, uncovered, for 30 minutes or until fruit is tender and mixture is thickened, stirring occasionally. Add hot pepper flakes, cinnamon, cloves, allspice and cayenne; boil gently for 5 minutes.
2. Remove hot jars from canner and ladle chutney into jars to within ½ inch (1 cm) of rim (headspace). Process 10 minutes for 1-cup (250 mL) jars as directed on page 14 (Easy Step-by-Step Preserving).

Makes 3 cups (750 mL).

Juniper Berry Chutney

This unusual chutney was inspired by a gift jar that Margaret's friend Janine brought her from Scotland. The flavor of juniper berries makes it a natural accompaniment to game, curry dishes and ham. Juniper berries are usually sold dry for flavoring meats, sauces and stuffings.

3	large tomatoes, peeled and chopped (about 2½ cups/625 mL)	3
1	large tart green apple, peeled, cored and chopped	1
1	medium onion, chopped	1
½ cup	sultana raisins	125 mL
½ cup	light brown sugar	125 mL
½ cup	each: liquid honey and cider vinegar	125 mL
¼ cup	water	50 mL
1 tbsp	juniper berries, crushed *(see Tip)*	15 mL
¼ tsp	salt	1 mL
⅛ tsp	hot pepper sauce	0.5 mL

1. Combine tomatoes, apple, onion, raisins, sugar, honey, vinegar, water and juniper berries in a large stainless steel or enamel saucepan. Bring to a boil over high heat, reduce heat and boil gently, uncovered, for 25 minutes or until thickened, stirring occasionally. Add salt and pepper sauce and cook for 2 minutes.
2. Remove hot jars from canner and ladle chutney into jars to within ½ inch (1 cm) of rim (headspace). Process 10 minutes for 1-cup (250 mL) jars and 15 minutes for 2-cup (500 mL) jars as directed on page 14 (Easy Step-by-Step Preserving).

Makes 4 cups (1 L).

tip | *Look for juniper berries in specialty or bulk stores carrying a selection of spices. Crushing the berries helps release their flavor.*

Mango Chutney

Mango Chutney is the one we think of as the "original" and most traditional of all chutneys. It goes well with curries, chicken, pork, lamb and game.

3	medium apples, peeled, cored and chopped	3
2	large mangoes, peeled and chopped	2
½	medium sweet red pepper, chopped	½
1½ cups	granulated sugar	375 mL
1 cup	finely chopped onion	250 mL
½ cup	golden raisins	125 mL
½ cup	white vinegar	125 mL
¼ cup	finely chopped peeled gingerroot	50 mL
1 tbsp	lemon juice	15 mL
2 tsp	curry powder	10 mL
½ tsp	each: ground nutmeg, cinnamon and salt	2 mL

1. Combine apples, mangoes, red pepper, sugar, onion, raisins, vinegar and gingerroot in a large stainless steel or enamel saucepan. Bring to a boil over high heat, reduce heat and boil gently, uncovered, for 20 minutes or until fruit is tender and mixture is thickened, stirring occasionally. Add lemon juice, curry powder, nutmeg, cinnamon and salt; boil gently for 5 minutes.
2. Remove hot jars from canner and ladle chutney into jars to within ½ inch (1 cm) of rim (headspace). Process 10 minutes for 1-cup (250 mL) jars and 15 minutes for 2-cup (500 mL) jars as directed on page 14 (Easy Step-by-Step Preserving).

Makes 5 cups (1.25 L).

Mango Papaya Chutney

These two magnificent tropical fruits, mango and papaya, make this chutney such a wonderful accompaniment to cottage cheese and fruit salad, or to any Caribbean chicken or pork dish. It is also excellent served with fish.

½ cup	granulated sugar	125 mL
¼ cup	water	50 mL
¼ cup	cider vinegar	50 mL
3 cups	finely chopped papaya and mango	750 mL
1–2 tbsp	minced jalapeño or hot yellow peppers	15–25 mL
1 tbsp	minced gingerroot	15 mL
½ tsp	ground coriander	2 mL
¼ tsp	salt	1 mL

1. Combine sugar and water in a heavy stainless steel or enamel saucepan. Bring to a boil, uncovered, over medium-high heat; reduce heat and boil gently for about 8 minutes or until mixture has become syrupy, without stirring.
2. Remove from heat and carefully add vinegar (mixture may bubble). Add papaya, mango, peppers, gingerroot, coriander and salt. Return to a boil, reduce heat to medium low and boil gently for 10 minutes or until fruit is tender and chutney has thickened, stirring occasionally.
3. Remove hot jars from canner and ladle chutney into jars to within ½ inch (1 cm) of rim (headspace). Process 10 minutes for 1-cup (250 mL) jars as directed on page 14 (Easy Step-by-Step Preserving).

Makes about 2¼ cups (550 mL).

Serving Suggestion:
Chutney Salad Dressing
Use 2–3 tbsp (25–45 mL) Mango Papaya Chutney with ⅓ cup (75 mL) low-fat plain yogurt as a dressing for torn romaine leaves.

Mixed Fruit Chutney

This zesty chutney was shared with us by Sheila Whyte of Thyme and Again Creative Catering and Take Home Foods in Ottawa and her chef, Robert Jutres. Robert created this recipe one fall when apples, pears and plums were abundant. It has become one of their best-sellers. Robert suggests serving it with grilled chicken and curries. He says, "Don't be tempted to taste it for at least 2 weeks. Allow the flavors to mellow."

6 cups	diced cored peeled tart apples (about 2 lb/1 kg)	1.5 L
3 cups	coarsely chopped peeled tomatoes (about 1 lb/500 g)	750 mL
2 cups	diced cored peeled firm pears (about 1 lb/500 g)	500 mL
1 cup	diced prune plums (about ½ lb/250 g)	250 mL
1 cup	raisins or currants	250 mL
5 cups	lightly packed dark brown sugar	1.25 L
2½ cups	cider or malt vinegar	625 mL
½ tsp	each: ground ginger, mace, ground cloves, cayenne pepper, coarsely ground black pepper and salt	2 mL

1. Combine apples, tomatoes, pears, plums and raisins in a large stainless steel or enamel saucepan. Stir in brown sugar, vinegar, ginger, mace, cloves, cayenne pepper, black pepper and salt.
2. Bring to a boil over high heat, stirring constantly. Reduce heat and boil gently for 1 hour or until chutney is very thick and golden brown, stirring frequently.
3. Remove hot jars from canner and ladle chutney into jars to within ½ inch (1 cm) of rim (headspace). Process 10 minutes for 1-cup (250 mL) jars and 15 minutes for 2-cup (500 mL) jars as directed on page 14 (Easy Step-by-Step Preserving).

Makes 4½ cups (1.125 L).

Orchard Chutney

Roasted garlic gives richness to this flavorful multi-fruit chutney that always adds interest to everyday meals. Served as an appetizer with soft Brie or Camembert cheese on crackers, it is quite magnificent!

2	heads garlic	2
2½ cups	chopped peeled tart apples (about 3 medium apples)	625 mL
2 cups	chopped peeled peaches (about 4 medium peaches)	500 mL
1 cup	chopped onions	250 mL
1 cup	golden raisins	250 mL
½ cup	chopped dried apricots	125 mL
1 cup	lightly packed brown sugar	250 mL
1¼ cups	cider vinegar	300 mL
¼ cup	balsamic vinegar	50 mL
1 tbsp	finely chopped gingerroot	15 mL
½ tsp	each: ground allspice and pickling salt	2 mL
¼ tsp	ground cloves	1 mL

1. Wrap each head of garlic in a double thickness of foil. Bake in a 400°C (200°C) oven for 40 minutes or until garlic is very soft. Cool and remove foil. With scissors, snip the tip from each clove and carefully squeeze out garlic, removing any pieces of the paper husk. Chop garlic paste finely with a knife.
2. Add garlic, apples, peaches, onions, raisins, apricots, sugar, vinegars, gingerroot, allspice, salt and cloves to a large stainless steel or enamel saucepan. Bring to a boil over high heat, reduce heat and boil gently, uncovered, for 30 minutes or until thickened.
3. Remove hot jars from canner and ladle chutney into jars to within ½ inch (1 cm) of rim (headspace). Process 10 minutes for 1-cup (250 mL) jars and 15 minutes for 2-cup (500 mL) jars as directed on page 14 (Easy Step-by-Step Preserving).

Makes 5½ cups (1.375 L).

Rhubarb, Date and Apricot Chutney

Dates and apricots give a rich flavor to the sweet-sour taste of rhubarb. It pairs especially well with ham, but also complements other dishes.

4 cups	sliced rhubarb	1 L
1 cup	chopped dried dates	250 mL
1 cup	lightly packed brown sugar	250 mL
½ cup	chopped dried apricots	125 mL
½ cup	cider vinegar	125 mL
¼ cup	finely chopped onion	50 mL
¼ cup	finely chopped Candied Ginger or crystallized ginger	50 mL
1 tsp	curry powder	5 mL
¼ tsp	ground nutmeg	1 mL
¼ tsp	pickling salt	1 mL

1. Combine rhubarb, dates, sugar, apricots, vinegar, onion, ginger, curry powder, nutmeg and salt in a medium stainless steel or enamel saucepan. Bring to a boil over medium-high heat; reduce heat and cook, uncovered, for 8 minutes, or until thickened and fruit is soft, stirring frequently.
2. Remove hot jars from canner and ladle chutney into jars to within ½ inch (1 cm) of rim (headspace). Process 10 minutes for 1-cup (250 mL) jars as directed on page 14 (Easy Step-by-Step Preserving).

Makes about 3 cups (750 mL).

Red Pepper Apricot Chutney

This light, fresh chutney goes well with pork curries, and with duck, poultry and lamb. Enjoy it in a Cheddar cheese sandwich or with cream cheese and melba toast. Wonderful plump Turkish apricots for this recipe are readily found in most food stores.

1 cup	diced sweet red pepper (about ½ large pepper)	250 mL
1 cup	chopped dried apricots	250 mL
¾ cup	chopped onion	175 mL
1 cup	apple, peeled, cored and chopped (about 1 apple)	250 mL
⅔ cup	granulated sugar	150 mL
½ cup	golden raisins	125 mL
½ cup	cider vinegar	125 mL
¼ cup	water	50 mL
1 tbsp	minced candied ginger	
	or crystallized ginger	15 mL
¼ tsp	each: ground cinnamon, mace and salt	1 mL
⅛ tsp	cayenne	0.5 mL

1. Combine red pepper, apricots, onion, apple, sugar, raisins, vinegar, water and ginger in a medium stainless steel or enamel saucepan. Bring to a boil over high heat, reduce heat, cover and boil gently for 10 minutes, stirring occasionally. Add cinnamon, mace, salt and cayenne. Cook, uncovered, for about 5 minutes, stirring frequently.
2. Remove hot jars from canner and ladle chutney into jars to within ½ inch (1 cm) of rim (headspace). Process 10 minutes for 1-cup (250 mL) jars as directed on page 14 (Easy Step-by-Step Preserving).

Makes about 2½ cups (625 mL).

Roasted Tomato Chutney

Roasting the ingredients gives this chutney a nice mellow, roasted taste that is unusual in chutneys. Serve on cooked pasta, with crackers, as an appetizer or in a pasta salad. It also matches well with grilled beef, chicken or pork. Since this chutney cannot be processed, it must be frozen for longer storage. So make lots and freeze it when plum tomatoes are in season and inexpensive.

1 cup	fresh coriander leaves, packed tightly	250 mL
10	plum tomatoes, quartered (about 2½ lb/1.25 kg)	10
10	cloves garlic, peeled	10
1	2-inch (5 cm) piece hot yellow or jalapeño pepper	1
2 tbsp	olive oil	25 mL
½ tsp	each: ground cumin, mustard seeds, salt and freshly ground pepper	2 mL

1. Place coriander in a shallow ovenproof casserole. Top with tomatoes, garlic and hot pepper. Drizzle with oil and sprinkle with seasonings.
2. Roast, uncovered, in a 350°F (180°C) oven for about 35 minutes. Remove from oven, stir to combine and cool slightly. Place in a food processor and pulse with on/off motion until coarsely chopped.
3. Spoon chutney into jars or plastic containers to within ½ inch (1 cm) of rim (headspace). Cover with tight-fitting lids. Label jars and refrigerate for up to 1 week or freeze for longer storage.

Makes 3 cups (750 mL).

Variation:
Fennel Seed Chutney
Replace mustard seeds with 1 tbsp (15 mL) fennel seeds in Step 1.

Sun-Dried Tomato Chutney

Two kinds of tomatoes, sun-dried and fresh, are used to create this exciting chutney. It has some spice level for further interest. Perfect with cooked rice, pasta, curries and egg and cheese dishes, it can also be served with grilled meats and chicken.

4	large tomatoes, peeled and chopped (about 3 cups/750 mL)	4
1 cup	finely chopped onion	250 mL
½ cup	chopped sun-dried tomatoes (not oil-packed)	125 mL
½ cup	dried currants	125 mL
½ cup	lightly packed brown sugar	125 mL
½ cup	water	125 mL
¼ cup	balsamic vinegar	50 mL
1	2-inch (5 cm) piece gingerroot, finely chopped	1
2	cloves garlic, minced	2
2 tsp	curry powder	10 mL
¼ tsp	each: salt and hot pepper flakes	1 mL

1. Combine tomatoes, onion, sun-dried tomatoes and currants in a large stainless steel or enamel saucepan. Stir in sugar, water, vinegar, gingerroot, garlic, curry powder, salt and pepper flakes.
2. Bring to a boil over high heat, stirring occasionally. Reduce heat to low and boil gently, uncovered, for 30 minutes or until chutney is very thick, stirring frequently.
3. Remove hot jars from canner and ladle chutney into jars to within ½ inch (1 cm) of rim (headspace). Process 10 minutes for 1-cup (250 mL) jars as directed on page 14 (Easy Step-by-Step Preserving).

Makes 3½ cups (875 mL).

All-Year Dried Fruit Chutney

All chutneys do not need to be prepared in the growing season. This one, using fruits available at any time of the year, is a marvelous addition to pork, poultry, beef and game. We have also used it as an appetizer with soft Brie or Camembert cheese on crackers.

1	large banana, mashed	1
1	large apple, peeled, cored and chopped	1
1	large red onion, chopped	1
3	cloves garlic, minced	3
½ cup	each: chopped dried apricots, prunes and dates	125 mL
⅓ cup	chopped mixed glacéed fruit	75 mL
2 tbsp	chopped minced Candied Ginger or crystallized ginger	25 mL
1 cup	cider vinegar	250 mL
½ cup	water	125 mL
½ tsp	each: cayenne, ground allspice, ground cardamom and salt	2 mL
1 cup	lightly packed dark brown sugar	250 mL

1. Combine banana, apple, onion, garlic, apricots, prunes, dates, glacéed fruit, ginger, vinegar and water in a large stainless steel or enamel saucepan. Bring to a boil over high heat, reduce heat and boil gently, uncovered, for 10 minutes, stirring occasionally. Add cayenne, allspice, cardamom, salt and sugar; boil gently, stirring occasionally, for 10 minutes or until thickened.
2. Remove hot jars from canner and ladle chutney into jars to within ½ inch (1 cm) of rim (headspace). Process 10 minutes for 1-cup (250 mL) jars and 15 minutes for 2-cup (500 mL) jars as directed on page 14 (Easy Step-by-Step Preserving).

Makes 4 cups (1 L).

Hellfire Chutney

Margaret's daughter Martha learned of this unusual chutney from someone who brought the recipe with her when she moved from India to Toronto. She generously shares it with us. You'll find it wonderful served with rice dishes and curries. But don't let the name frighten you. You control the amount of spicing and the resulting hellfire.

1 lb	pitted dates, cut up	500 g
1¾ cups	white vinegar, divided	425 mL
¾ cup	granulated sugar	175 mL
½–1 tsp	cayenne pepper	2–5 mL
¾ tsp	each: ground cinnamon and ground ginger	4 mL
¼ tsp	each: ground cloves and salt	1 mL
3 tbsp	liquid honey	45 mL

1. Place dates in a large stainless steel or enamel saucepan with 1½ cups (375 mL) vinegar and allow to soak for 30 minutes. Bring to a boil over medium-high heat, reduce heat to low and cook, covered, for 10 minutes or until dates are tender. Remove from heat and cool. Place in a food processor and purée until smooth.
2. Return mixture to saucepan; add sugar, cayenne, cinnamon, ginger, cloves, salt, honey and remaining ¼ cup (50 mL) vinegar. Cook, uncovered, over low heat until hot, about 5 minutes, stirring constantly.
3. Remove hot jars from canner and ladle chutney into jars to within ½ inch (1 cm) of rim (headspace). Process 10 minutes for 1-cup (250 mL) jars as directed on page 14 (Easy Step-by-Step Preserving).

Makes 3½ cups (875 mL).

chapter 10

SAVORY SAUCES

S AUCES add zest to foods. Tomato sauces, chili sauces, mustards as
well as unusual piquant sauces each give their own special nuance
to the foods they accompany.

Chili sauces are ketchup-like spicy sauces but with a coarser
consistency. They are made with tomatoes, onions, green peppers, chile
peppers or chili powder, vinegar, sugar and spices. Asian cooking uses
many appealing sauces to accompany a great variety of dishes. Enjoy
our easily prepared Asian Plum Sauce (page 247) and Thai Chili Sauce
(page 249).

The pungent flavor of mustard seed has been enhancing food since
early Greek and Roman days. The Romans carried mustard north to
England, and no English kitchen has since been without it. The French
combined mustard seed with white wine and spices to create the classic
Dijon blend, as in Dijon-Style Mustard (page 232).

You can influence the sharpness of the mustard you make by
changing the liquid you use. Mixing mustard with water produces the
hottest, sharpest taste by releasing an enzyme in the seed that frees
the fiery compounds. Acids such as vinegar or wine give a much milder
flavor. Vinegar is used in English-style mustard, Champagne or white
wine in Dijon-style mustard, and flat beer is often used by the Chinese.
Different kinds of seeds also have different flavors. The darker seeds
have a more pungent aroma and flavor.

List of Recipes: Savory Sauces

Mustards

Mustard has been used since Roman times and commercial makers offer us many varieties. The mustard seed is usually ground before being mixed with a liquid to mellow its natural bitterness. Then the mustard is cooked at length to decrease the pungency and aged to develop the flavors.

Basic Coarse Mustard

Using mustard seeds instead of mustard powder gives the interesting coarse texture to this condiment. This recipe can be used in its basic form or in its several variations.

⅓ cup	mustard seeds	75 mL
⅓ cup	cider vinegar	75 mL
1	clove garlic, halved	1
3 tbsp	water	45 mL
3 tbsp	liquid honey	45 mL
¼ tsp	salt	1 mL
⅛ tsp	ground cinnamon	0.5 mL

1. Combine mustard seeds, vinegar and garlic in a small bowl. Cover and refrigerate for 36 hours.
2. Discard garlic. Process mixture in a food processor with water until coarse consistency. Stir in honey, salt and cinnamon.
3. Divide mixture into 3 equal parts and proceed as below.

Horseradish Mustard: To one part, add 1 tsp (5 mL) horseradish.
Peppercorn Mustard: To one part, add 1 tsp (5 mL) green peppercorns, crushed.
Herb Mustard: To one part, add ¼ tsp (1 mL) or more as desired of any dried herb. (Try tarragon, dill, thyme, basil or oregano).

Refrigerate in tightly sealed containers.

Makes ¼ cup (50 mL) of each.

Serving Suggestions:
Try this on sandwiches with cold cuts, ham or roast beef.
Add ⅓ cup (75 mL) mayonnaise to 2 tbsp (25 mL) Basic Coarse Mustard.

Makes about ½ cup (125 mL).

Creamy Mustard Sauce
Use on cooked vegetables, to top baked potatoes and to dress a cab-bage or tossed green salad.
To ¼ cup (50 mL) Horseradish Mustard, add ½ cup (125 mL) light sour cream, 2 tbsp (25 mL) lemon juice and 2 tbsp (25 mL) chopped fresh parsley.

Makes about ¾ cup (175 mL).

Wine Mustard

Legend has it that a vinegar and mustard maker in Dijon first added wine to his mustard in the 1700s, and so began the resurgence of mustards in Europe.

½ cup	liquid honey	125 mL
⅓ cup	white wine	75 mL
¼ cup	dry mustard	50 mL
1	egg	1
1 tbsp	vegetable oil	15 mL
1 tsp	all-purpose flour	5 mL

1. Combine honey, wine and dry mustard in a small saucepan. Whisk in egg, oil and flour; cook over medium heat for 2 to 3 minutes or until bubbly, stirring constantly. Cook for 1 minute longer, stirring constantly. Remove from heat.
2. Cool to room temperature. Cover and refrigerate in a tightly sealed container for up to 2 weeks.

Makes 1 cup (250 mL).

Dijon-Style Mustard

This smooth, flavorful mustard compares well to fine commercial Dijon mustards. And it's easy and quick to make. Increase the amount of hot pepper sauce if you want your mustard to have more bite. Mix it with your favorite jam for a sweet and tangy sauce that is perfect for dipping or spreading on meat before broiling. Use it to make the specialty sauces described below. With little effort you can have a refrigerator full of fancy mustards.

¾ cup	dry white wine	175 mL
¼ cup	chopped onion	50 mL
1	small clove garlic, minced	1
½ cup	dry mustard	125 mL
1 tbsp	each: liquid honey and canola oil	15 mL
½ tsp	salt	2 mL
2–3 drops	hot pepper sauce	2–3 drops

1. Combine wine, onion and garlic in a small saucepan. Bring to a boil over high heat, reduce heat and boil gently, uncovered, for 5 minutes. Strain and discard solids.
2. Whisk wine into mustard in a small bowl until well blended. Return to saucepan; add honey, oil, salt and pepper sauce. Bring to a boil and boil gently for 10 minutes to blend flavors and thicken slightly, stirring frequently. Store in a tightly sealed container in the refrigerator for up to 1 month.

Makes ⅔ cup (150 mL).

More Serving Suggestions:

Raspberry Mustard Sauce

Use Dijon-Style Mustard to make this wonderful sauce full of the essence of raspberries. Serve it with ham and, of course, use it to complement the taste of roast pork.

Combine ½ cup (125 mL) Dijon-Style Mustard, 1 tbsp (15 mL) Red Wine Raspberry Vinegar (page 259), ¼ cup (50 mL) crushed raspberries and 2 tsp (10 mL) granulated sugar. Stir well to combine. Store in a tightly sealed container in the refrigerator for up to 1 week.

Makes ¾ cup (175 mL).

Savory Mustard Sauce

Parsley and oregano transform Dijon-Style Mustard into a superb sauce to spread on any kind of meat or cheese sandwich.

Combine ¼ cup (50 mL) Dijon-Style Mustard, 2 tsp (10 mL) chopped fresh parsley, 1 tsp (5 mL) chopped fresh oregano, ½ tsp (2 mL) each: lemon juice and grated lemon rind. Store in a tightly sealed container in the refrigerator for up to two weeks.

Makes ¼ cup (50 mL).

Mustard Fruit Dip

Wonderful as a dip for cooked shrimp or chicken cubes.

Combine 2 tbsp (25 mL) Dijon-Style Mustard, ¼ cup (50 mL) chutney and 2 tsp (10 mL) lemon juice.

Makes ⅓ cup (75 mL).

Sun-Dried Tomato Mustard

The subtle sun-dried tomato flavor and interesting coarse texture of
this mustard gives a meal extra "zip."

¼ cup	mustard seeds	50 mL
½ cup	chopped sun-dried tomatoes	
	(not oil-packed)	125 mL
¼ cup	balsamic vinegar	50 mL
2 tbsp	dry mustard	25 mL
2 tbsp	extra virgin olive oil	25 mL
1 tsp	salt	5 mL
½ tsp	granulated sugar	2 mL

Cover mustard seeds with warm water and refrigerate overnight. Drain
and rinse seeds. Place mustard seeds, tomatoes, vinegar, dry mustard,
oil, salt and sugar in a food processor. Process until almost smooth
and thickened. Store in a tightly sealed container in the refrigerator
for up to 1 month or freeze for longer storage.

Makes about 1 cup (250 mL).

Old-Style Whole Seed Mustard

Yellow or brown mustard seeds may be used in this grainy home-style mustard. The brown seeds have a more pungent aroma and flavor than their yellow cousins.

¼ cup	yellow mustard seeds	50 mL
¼ cup	brown mustard seeds	50 mL
½ cup	white wine vinegar	125 mL
1	bay leaf	1
1 tbsp	each: liquid honey and canola oil	15 mL
¼ tsp	salt	1 mL

Combine mustard seeds, vinegar and bay leaf and refrigerate for 24 hours. Remove bay leaf and discard. Place seeds and their liquid, honey, oil and salt in a food processor. Process until seeds are broken and mustard is pasty. Store in a tightly sealed container in the refrigerator for up to 1 month or freeze for longer storage.

Makes about 1 cup (250 mL).

tip | *The liquid used to soak the seeds is important to the taste of the mustard. Vinegar gives a mustard with a mild flavor. For a sharper taste, use water to replace the vinegar. Water releases an enzyme that reacts with compounds in the seeds to produce the sharp mustard oils. You can also replace vinegar with your favorite wine for a spicier taste or with beer for an extremely hot bite.*

Your Basic Multi-Use Tomato Sauce

This fabulous tomato-rich sauce is made with three kinds of tomatoes, sun-dried, plum and regular. We like to add it to soups and beef stews for a nice flavor boost.

10	plum tomatoes, peeled and chopped (about 2½ lb/1.25 kg)	10
10	large tomatoes, peeled and chopped (about 4 lb/2 kg)	10
4	large cloves garlic, minced	4
2	large stalks celery, chopped	2
2	medium carrots, chopped	2
1	large onion, chopped	1
1	large zucchini, chopped	1
1	large sweet green pepper, chopped	1
½ cup	sun-dried tomatoes	125 mL
⅔ cup	dry red wine	150 mL
½ cup	red wine vinegar	125 mL
2	bay leaves	2
1 tbsp	pickling salt	15 mL
2 tsp	each: dried oregano and basil	10 mL
1 tsp	granulated sugar	5 mL
¼ tsp	each: ground cinnamon and pepper	2 mL
¼ cup	chopped fresh parsley	50 mL

1. Combine tomatoes, garlic, celery, carrots, onion, zucchini and green pepper in a very large stainless steel or enamel saucepan. Add 1 cup (250 mL) water. Bring to a boil over high heat, reduce heat and boil gently, covered, for 25 minutes or until mixture begins to thicken, stirring occasionally.

2. Soak sun-dried tomatoes in boiling water until softened. Drain and dice. Add to sauce with wine, vinegar, bay leaves, salt, oregano, basil, sugar, cinnamon and pepper. Continue to boil gently until desired consistency, stirring frequently. Discard bay leaves and stir in parsley.

3. Remove hot jars from canner and ladle sauce into jars to within ½ inch (1 cm) of rim (headspace). Process 35 minutes for 2-cup (500 mL) jars and 40 minutes for 4-cup (1 L) jars as directed on page 14 (Easy Step-by-Step Preserving).

Makes 12 cups (3 L).

Seasoned Tomato Sauce

Whenever there is an abundance of tomatoes, it's time to make this fresh tasting basic sauce. And since the tomatoes are not peeled before cooking, it is quick to make. Use it anytime a tomato sauce is called for—in pasta sauces, soups, stews, pizzas or casseroles.

12 cups	chopped ripe plum tomatoes	3 L
	(about 6 lb/3 kg), unpeeled	
1 cup	chopped onion	250 mL
2	cloves garlic, minced	2
2 tbsp	chopped fresh oregano or 1 tsp (5 mL) dried	25 mL
1 tsp	granulated sugar	5 mL
½ tsp	freshly ground black pepper	2 mL
2	bay leaves	2
2 tbsp	red wine vinegar or lemon juice	25 mL
½ tsp	pickling salt	2 mL

1. Combine tomatoes, onion, garlic, oregano, sugar, pepper and bay leaves in a large stainless steel or enamel saucepan. Bring to a boil over high heat, reduce heat and boil gently, uncovered, stirring occasionally, for 1 ¼ hours or until very thick. Press through a food mill or coarse sieve; remove and discard seeds and skins. Add vinegar and salt to pulp.
2. Remove hot jars from canner and ladle sauce into jars to within ½ inch (1 cm) of rim (headspace). Process for 35 minutes for 1-cup (250 mL) and 2-cup (500 mL) jars as directed on page 14 (Easy Step-by-Step Preserving).

Makes about 7 cups (1.75 L).

Summer Sizzle Barbecue Sauce

Whether served with beef, chicken and pork, or humble burgers and hot dogs, this barbecue sauce gives meat a real sizzle. When grilling season arrives or in households where it's year round, this is a very valuable sauce to have on hand.

2 tbsp	canola oil	25 mL
2	medium onions, chopped	2
2	large cloves garlic, minced	2
4	large tomatoes, peeled and finely chopped (about 3 cups/750 mL)	4
½ cup	dry red wine or beef broth	125 mL
3 tbsp	liquid honey	45 mL
1 tbsp	each: Worcestershire sauce and cider vinegar	15 mL
1 tsp	each: dry mustard and green peppercorns	5 mL
½ tsp	each: chili powder and salt	2 mL
½ cup	tomato sauce	125 mL
1 tbsp	brown sugar	15 mL
¼ tsp	hot pepper sauce	1 mL

1. Heat oil in a medium stainless steel or enamel saucepan over medium-high heat. Add onions and garlic and sauté for 5 minutes or until tender, stirring frequently.
2. Add tomatoes, wine, honey, Worcestershire sauce, vinegar, mustard, peppercorns, chile powder and salt. Bring to a boil, reduce heat and boil gently, uncovered, for 30 minutes or until thickened. Remove from heat and purée in a food processor or blender until smooth. Stir in tomato sauce, sugar and pepper sauce, return to saucepan and bring to a boil.
3. Remove hot jars from canner and ladle sauce into jars to within ½ inch (1 cm) of rim (headspace). Process 20 minutes for 1-cup (250 mL) jars as directed on page 14 (Easy Step-by-Step Preserving).

Makes 3 cups (750 mL).

Chunky Basil Pasta Sauce

Fall is the time to turn the rich flavors of field-ripened tomatoes and fresh basil into a delicious sauce to have on hand during the winter months. We love it served on fresh pasta and topped with freshly grated Parmesan cheese.

8 cups	coarsely chopped peeled tomatoes (about 9–12 tomatoes or 4 lb/2 kg)	2 L
1 cup	chopped onion	250 mL
3	cloves garlic, minced	3
⅔ cup	red wine	150 mL
⅓ cup	red wine vinegar	75 mL
½ cup	chopped fresh basil	125 mL
1 tbsp	chopped fresh parsley	15 mL
1 tsp	pickling salt	5 mL
½ tsp	granulated sugar	2 mL
1	can (6 oz/156 mL) tomato paste	1

1. Combine tomatoes, onion, garlic, wine, vinegar, basil, parsley, salt, sugar and tomato paste in a very large stainless steel or enamel saucepan. Bring to a boil over high heat, reduce heat to low and simmer, uncovered, for 40 minutes or until mixture reaches desired consistency, stirring frequently.
2. Remove hot jars from canner and ladle sauce into jars to within ½ inch (1 cm) of rim (headspace). Process 35 minutes for 2-cup (500 mL) jars and 40 minutes for 4-cup (1 L) jars as directed on page 14 (Easy Step-by-Step Preserving).

Makes 8 cups (2 L).

Cherries

Tomato salsa

Fruit jams

Coarse mustard

Roasted Vegetable Pasta Sauce

Roasting vegetables for this full-flavored tomato sauce changes a few simple ingredients into an epicurean treat. Serve with linguine or other pasta and a generous sprinkling of freshly grated Parmigiano-Reggiano cheese.

10	plum tomatoes, unpeeled (about 2½ lb/1.25 kg)	10
4	cloves garlic, unpeeled	4
2	small onions, unpeeled	2
1	sweet red pepper	1
¼ cup	balsamic vinegar	50 mL
1 tbsp	chopped fresh oregano or 1 tsp (5 mL) dried	15 mL
1 tsp	granulated sugar	5 mL
1 tsp	salt	5 mL

1. Place tomatoes, garlic, onions and red pepper on a lightly greased baking sheet. Roast in a 450°F (230°C) oven for 45 minutes, removing the garlic after 12 to 15 minutes or when soft. Remove remaining vegetables when they are soft and the skins blistered. Let stand until cool enough to handle.
2. Peel tomatoes, being careful to catch all the juice. Squeeze garlic and onions to remove soft centers. Peel and seed pepper. Place all vegetables in a food processor; process until smooth.
3. Place vegetable purée in a large stainless steel or enamel sauce-pan. Add vinegar, oregano, sugar and salt. Bring to a boil over high heat, reduce heat and boil, uncovered for about 15 minutes, or until the mixtures achieves desired consistency, stirring frequently.
4. Remove hot jars from canner and ladle sauce into jars to within ½ inch (1 cm) of rim (headspace). Process 35 minutes for 2-cup (500 mL) jars and 40 minutes for 4-cup (1 L) jars as directed on page 14 (Easy Step-by-Step Preserving).

Makes 3½ cups (875 mL).

Grandma's Chili Sauce

There are probably as many recipes for chili sauce as there are grand-mothers. We especially like this recipe, shared with us by a home economist. It was her grandmother's specialty.

4 cups	diced peeled tomatoes (about 2 lb/1 kg)	1 L
5	stalks celery, finely diced	5
2	apples, peeled, cored and diced	2
1	small sweet green pepper, seeded and finely diced	1
1	small hot red pepper, seeded and finely chopped	1
1	small onion, finely chopped	1
½	sweet red pepper, seeded and finely diced	½
1 cup	white vinegar	250 mL
⅓ cup	granulated sugar	75 mL
½ tsp	pickling salt	2 mL
3	cinnamon sticks, each 3 inches (8 cm) long	3
1	1-inch (2.5 cm) piece dried whole ginger	1
1 tsp	whole allspice berries	5 mL

1. Place tomatoes, celery, apples, green pepper, hot pepper, onion, red pepper, vinegar, sugar and salt in a large stainless steel or enamel saucepan.
2. Tie cinnamon, ginger and allspice in a small square of cheesecloth. Add to vegetables. Bring to a boil over high heat, reduce heat and boil gently, uncovered, for about 1½ hours or until mixture is thick, stirring occasionally. Discard spice bag.
3. Remove hot jars from canner and ladle sauce into jars to within ½ inch (1 cm) of rim (headspace). Process 15 minutes for 1-cup (250 mL) jars and 20 minutes for 2-cup (500 mL) jars as directed on page 14 (Easy Step-by-Step Preserving).

Makes 4 cups (1 L).

Fruit Chili Sauce

This traditional relish originates from the fruit-growing regions of Canada where peaches and pears are abundant in the fall.

6 cups	chopped peeled tomatoes (about 3 lb/1.5 kg)	1.5 L
2 cups	finely chopped onions	500 mL
2 cups	each: chopped peeled peaches, pears and apples	500 mL
1 cup	finely chopped celery	250 mL
2	sweet green peppers, finely chopped	2
1	sweet or hot red pepper, seeded and finely chopped	1
1½ cups	white or cider vinegar	375 mL
1 tbsp	pickling spice	15 mL
2 tsp	pickling salt	10 mL
2 cups	granulated sugar	500 mL

1. Combine tomatoes, onions, peaches, pears, apples, celery, green and red peppers and vinegar in a very large stainless steel or enamel saucepan. Place pickling spice in a tea ball or tie in a piece of cheesecloth. Add spice and salt to saucepan. Bring to a boil over high heat, reduce heat and boil gently, uncovered, for 1 hour or until thick, stirring occasionally.
2. Stir in sugar. Return to a boil and boil gently for 30 minutes, stirring occasionally. Remove spice bag.
3. Remove hot jars from canner and ladle sauce into jars to within ½ inch (1 cm) of rim (headspace). Process 15 minutes for 1-cup (250 mL) jars and 20 minutes for 2-cup (500 mL) jars as directed on page 14 (Easy Step-by-Step Preserving).

Makes 8 cups (2 L).

Mango Chile Sauce

Mangoes, pineapple juice, rice vinegar and gingerroot blend with traditional ingredients in this flavorful sauce. Use it as you would use the traditional sauce. It does wonders to dress up a plain meat loaf.

3 cups	coarsely chopped peeled plum tomatoes (about 6–8 tomatoes or 1½ lb/750 g)	750 mL
2 cups	chopped mango (about 3 mangoes)	500 mL
1	small hot red chile, seeded and finely chopped	1
¾ cup	rice vinegar	175 mL
½ cup	pineapple juice	125 mL
½ cup	each: chopped onion and celery	125 mL
1 tbsp	minced gingerroot	15 mL
3	whole cloves	3
1	bay leaf	1
⅓ cup	granulated sugar	75 mL
½ tsp	pickling salt	2 mL

1. Combine tomatoes, mango, chile, vinegar, pineapple juice, onion, celery, gingerroot, cloves and bay leaf in a large stainless steel or enamel saucepan. Bring to a boil over high heat, reduce heat and boil gently, uncovered, for 1 hour or until thickened, stirring occasionally.

2. Add sugar and salt; return to a boil and boil gently for 10 minutes. Remove and discard bay leaf and cloves.

3. Remove hot jars from canner and ladle sauce into jars to within ½ inch (1 cm) of rim (headspace). Process 15 minutes for 1-cup (250 mL) jars and 20 minutes for 2-cup (500 mL) jars as directed on page 14 (Easy Step-by-Step Preserving).

Makes 4½ cups (1.125 L).

Blender Ketchup

If you thought ketchup was only for kids, try this adult version and you'll change your mind. Our Blender Ketchup is less sweet and has a fresher tomato flavor than commercial ketchups. It adds zest to casseroles, soups and meat loaves.

8 cups	coarsely chopped unpeeled plum tomatoes, about (4 lb/2 kg)	2 L
½ cup	chopped onion	125 mL
½ cup	chopped sweet red pepper	125 mL
⅔ cup	cider vinegar	150 mL
¼ cup	granulated sugar	50 mL
2 tsp	pickling salt	10 mL
1	cinnamon stick, 2 inches (5 cm) long	1
½ tsp	each: whole allspice, whole cloves, peppercorns	2 mL
1	bay leaf	1

1. Process tomatoes, onion and red pepper in a blender or food processor until smooth. Remove to a large stainless steel or enamel saucepan. Add vinegar and bring to a boil over high heat, reduce heat and boil gently, uncovered, for 30 minutes.
2. Add sugar and salt. Tie cinnamon, allspice, cloves, peppercorns and bay leaf in cheesecloth and add to saucepan. Return to a boil and boil gently, uncovered, stirring frequently, until volume is reduced by half or until mixture rounds up on a spoon without separation, about 1½ hours. Discard spice..
3. Remove hot jars from canner and ladle ketchup into jars to within ½ inch (1 cm) of rim (headspace). Process 15 minutes for 1-cup (250 mL) jars as directed on page 14 (Easy Step-by-Step Preserving).

Makes about 4 cups (1 L).

Microwave Mango Ketchup

Ketchup hasn't always been made from tomatoes. This popular condiment originated in seventeenth-century China, when it was made of
spicy pickled fish. British seamen took it home and later added tomatoes, making the blend we know today. Try this interesting version on
chicken or beef burgers or blackened fish.

2	mangoes, peeled and finely chopped	2
¼ cup	granulated sugar	50 mL
¼ cup	dry white wine	50 mL
¼ cup	cider vinegar	50 mL
1 tsp	ground ginger	5 mL
½ tsp	salt	2 mL
¼ tsp	each: ground allspice and cloves	1 mL

1. Combine mangoes, sugar, wine, vinegar, ginger, salt, allspice and
   cloves in a medium microwavable container. Microwave, uncovered, on High (100%) for 5 minutes. Stir.
2. Microwave on Low (30%) for 3 to 5 minutes or until mixture is
   very thick, stirring several times.
3. Remove hot jars from canner and ladle ketchup into jars to within
   ½ inch (1 cm) of rim (headspace). Process 15 minutes for 1-cup
   (250 mL) jars as directed on page 14 (Easy Step-by-Step Preserving).

Makes 2 cups (500 mL).

Asian Plum Sauce

Sauces of this type are not only difficult to find but often expensive. The Asian flavors complement roast pork, meatballs and of course such Oriental foods as spring and egg rolls. Margaret's daughter Janice, who gave us this recipe, uses it as a dipping sauce for cheese bites and sausage rolls.

9	purple plums, washed and pitted (about 1½ lb/750 g)	9
1½ cups	firmly packed brown sugar	375 mL
1 cup	cider vinegar	250 mL
1½ tsp	salt	7 mL
1½ cups	finely chopped onion	375 mL
3	cloves garlic, crushed	3
¼ cup	raisins	50 mL
2 tsp	soy sauce	10 mL
¼ tsp	chili powder	1 mL
⅛ tsp	each: ground cloves, cinnamon, ginger and allspice	0.5 mL

1. Finely chop plums in a food processor or by hand. You should have about 1¾ cups (425 mL).
2. Combine plums, sugar, vinegar and salt in a large stainless steel or enamel saucepan. Bring to a boil over high heat and boil gently, uncovered, for 3 minutes, stirring occasionally.
3. Add onion, garlic, raisins, soy sauce, chili powder, cloves, cinnamon, ginger and allspice to saucepan. Return to a boil, reduce heat and boil gently, uncovered, for 45 minutes or until mixture is thickened, stirring occasionally.
4. Remove hot jars from canner and ladle sauce into jars to within ½ inch (1 cm) of rim (headspace). Process 15 minutes for 1-cup (250 mL) jars as directed on page 14 (Easy Step-by-Step Preserving).

Makes 3½ cups (875 mL).

Asian Whisky Sauce

Margaret has been using this seafood sauce and marinade since time immemorial, or so it seems. And it never fails to please everyone who tastes it. She uses it for marinating fish fillets as well as whole fish, chicken and pork.

¼ cup	each: canola oil and soy sauce	50 mL
2	cloves garlic, minced	2
½ cup	rye whisky	125 mL
4 tsp	brown sugar	20 mL
¼ tsp	freshly ground pepper	1 mL
	small piece gingerroot, peeled and chopped (optional)	

1. Combine oil, soy sauce, garlic, rye whisky, sugar, pepper and gingerroot (if using) in a tightly sealed container, shake to blend well. Refrigerate until ready to use.

Makes 1 cup (250 mL).

Use about ⅓ cup (75 mL) of Asian Whisky Sauce to marinate 4 chicken breasts or drumsticks or about 1 lb (500 g) fish or pork. Any unused sauce may be stored in the refrigerator for up to 1 month.

Serving Suggestions:
Asian Salmon

Place 4 salmon steaks or 2 fillets in a resealable plastic bag. Pour ½ cup (125 mL) Asian Whisky Sauce over salmon, seal the bag and turn to coat the food evenly. Refrigerate for 1 to 2 hours, turning bag occasionally. Remove salmon from the marinade and grill or broil. Bring the remaining marinade to a boil for 5 minutes, then use to brush on salmon during the cooking.

Makes 4 servings.

Thai Chili Sauce

Thai flavors of fish sauce, lime and garlic combine to make this amazing sauce to serve with fish or chicken.

1	small tomato, chopped	1
½	small sweet red pepper, seeded and chopped	½
½ cup	chopped onion	125 mL
1	clove garlic, minced	1
3 tbsp	minced gingerroot	45 mL
½ cup	chicken stock	125 mL
⅓ cup	fish sauce	75 mL
3 tbsp	lime juice	45 mL
2 tbsp	each: brown sugar and rice vinegar	25 mL
2 tsp	hot pepper flakes	10 mL
¼ cup	chopped fresh coriander	50 mL

1. Combine tomato, pepper, onion, garlic, gingerroot, chicken stock, fish sauce, lime juice, sugar, vinegar and hot pepper flakes in a medium saucepan. Bring to a boil over high heat, reduce heat and boil gently, uncovered, for 10 minutes. Remove from heat and stir in coriander.
2. Remove hot jars from canner and ladle sauce into jars to within ½ inch (1 cm) of rim (headspace). Process 15 minutes for 1-cup (250 mL) jars as directed on page 14 (Easy Step-by-Step Preserving).

Makes 2 cups (500 mL).

Serving Suggestion:
Thai Baked Fish
Spread several spoonfuls of Thai Chili Sauce over fish fillets such as orange roughy, halibut or salmon. Bake in a 400°F (200°C) oven for 12 minutes or until fish is opaque and flakes easily with a fork. Serve with additional sauce.

Cranberry Sauce with Spirit

There will be no going back to traditional cranberry sauce once you have tried cranberries cooked with port wine.

1 cup	granulated sugar	250 mL
¼ cup	water	50 mL
1 tbsp	red wine vinegar	15 mL
2½ cups	fresh or frozen cranberries	625 mL
½ cup	port	125 mL
2	cinnamon sticks, each 3 inches long (8 cm)	2

1. Combine sugar, water and vinegar in a medium stainless steel or enamel saucepan. Bring to a boil over high heat, stirring to dissolve sugar. Add cranberries; return to a boil, reduce heat and boil gently, uncovered, for 5 minutes, stirring frequently. Stir in port.
2. Remove hot jars from canner and place a cinnamon stick in each jar. Ladle sauce into jars to within ½ inch (1 cm) of rim (headspace). Process 15 minutes for 1-cup (250 mL) jars as directed on page 14 (Easy Step-by-Step Preserving).

Makes 2 cups (500 mL).

Herbed Raspberry and Red Currant Sauce

This great fruit combo provides lots of flavor interest to grilled or barbecued chicken breasts and pork chops. Stirred into plain yogurt, it makes an excellent fruit salad topping.

2 cups	fresh or frozen unsweetened raspberries	500 mL
2 cups	fresh or frozen red currants	500 mL
½ cup	water	125 mL
1½ cups	granulated sugar	375 mL
½ tsp	each: dried tarragon and thyme	2 mL

1. Combine raspberries, currants and water in a medium stainless steel or enamel saucepan. Bring to a boil over high heat, reduce heat and boil gently, covered, for 20 minutes. Strain mixture through a fine sieve or cloth; discard pulp.
2. Return sauce to pan, return to a boil and slowly add sugar, stirring constantly until sugar is dissolved. Stir in tarragon and thyme; boil gently for 5 minutes.
3. Remove hot jars from canner and ladle sauce into jars to within ½ inch (1 cm) of rim (headspace). Process 15 minutes for 1-cup (250 mL) jars as directed on page 14 (Easy Step-by-Step Preserving).

Makes 3 cups (750 mL).

Indonesian Satay Sauce

Fabulous as a sauce for pork kabobs or satays, this sauce also makes a delightful dip for raw vegetables.

2 tsp	vegetable oil	10 mL
1 cup	finely chopped onion	250 mL
4	cloves garlic, minced	4
⅔ cup	cider vinegar	150 mL
½ cup	each: molasses and soy sauce	125 mL
2 tsp	hot pepper flakes	10 mL
2 tsp	minced peeled gingerroot	10 mL
½ cup	peanut butter	125 mL

1. Heat oil in a nonstick saucepan over medium-high heat and sauté onion and garlic for 3 minutes or until tender, stirring frequently.
2. Add vinegar, molasses, soy sauce, hot pepper flakes and gingerroot. Bring to a boil, reduce heat and boil gently for 5 minutes. Blend in peanut butter; boil gently for 1 minute.
3. Remove hot jars from canner and ladle sauce into jars to within ½ inch (1 cm) of rim. Process 20 minutes for 1-cup (250 mL) jars as directed on page 14 (Easy Step-by-Step Preserving).

Makes 2 cups (500 mL).

Serving Suggestion:
Chicken Barbecued with Indonesian Satay Sauce
Indonesian Satay Sauce imparts a rich glaze to chicken. For faster barbecuing, microwave chicken on Medium (50%) until partially cooked before placing on hot grill.

Marinate chicken pieces in Indonesian Satay Sauce, covered, for 1 hour at room temperature or up to 6 hours in refrigerator. Remove chicken from marinade, reserving marinade. Boil marinade for 5 minutes. Place chicken on hot barbecue grill. Cook on low heat for 45 minutes, turning several times and basting with hot marinade. Alternatively, arrange chicken in a single layer on a foil-lined baking dish. Bake in a 375°F (190°C) oven for 30 to 35 minutes. Discard any leftover marinade.

chapter 11

FLAVORED OILS AND SPECIALTY VINEGARS

FLAVORED oils and specialty vinegars are currently riding a wave of popularity as a way to enhance the taste of many foods. And because they are so highly flavored, just a little goes a long way. We love to have them on hand for making a simple vinaigrette, for livening up a marinade or for drizzling over steamed vegetables.

Flavored Oils

Flavored oils are made by infusing the essence of such foods as garlic, herbs or chile peppers into an oil. We are excited about our new Nut-Infused Oils. You can make a variety of exotic nut oils at a fraction of the expense of the commercial ones.

Flavored oils pack a lot of flavor into just a few drops. They are an excellent way to lower the amount of fat in your diet. Little effort is needed to make these versatile condiments. But be sure to follow the instructions carefully and make note of the Food Safety Alert, for if these oils are not made and stored properly, there can be a risk of botulism. Then enjoy the wonderful flavors oils offer with no concern for their safety.

The problem with infusing oils with fresh foods is Clostridium botulinum spores. Although found widely on foods, the spores are seldom a concern because they find few conditions where they can grow. However, whenever a fresh food, such as garlic, is immersed in oil and kept at temperatures over 50°F (10°C), the food provides enough moisture to enable the spores to grow and produce a potentially fatal toxin. Any oil with a flavoring essence, such as herbs, garlic or fresh peppers, should be heated at a low oven temperature (300°F/150°C) for a specified time. This process, which has been confirmed by Health Canada, drives off the water that is in the food and has an additional advantage of speeding up the infusion of the flavor from the food into the oil. The oil is then strained and put into bottles. After proper processing, flavored oils need to be kept refrigerated for safety and to prolong their flavor.

When making the oils, we use a 2-cup (500 mL) glass measuring cup or a clean 28-oz (796 mL) can with the lid removed. Follow the recipe instructions carefully and be sure not to increase the amount of foods you add to the oil, because the heating time is based on the amounts in the recipe. Check that the finished oil is clear and the vegetables blackened. After the oil is strained, if it is cloudy or if there is a separate layer at the bottom of the bottle, the oil was not heated long enough and must be heated until it becomes clear, or it can be refrigerated and used within a week.

Canola, a neutral-tasting oil, is perfect for letting the flavor of added foods come through. However, you may prefer to make the oils using extra virgin olive for the unique taste it provides. Olive oil becomes cloudy with refrigerator storage, but when the oil is slightly warmed, this cloudiness disappears. Just remember with any flavored oil not to leave it at room temperature for longer than 1 hour and to discard any oil that has sat out for a longer time.

Specialty Vinegars

Vinegars are a fundamental part of any good cook's pantry. Yet many are very expensive. Share our enjoyment of these economical, easy-to-prepare homemade vinegars to enliven a dressing for a tossed green salad, add sparkle to steamed vegetables and transform a meat or poultry marinade into something memorable.

Specialty vinegars are incredibly easy to make because the high acid level of vinegar prevents the growth of the botulism organism and eliminates any need to process them in a hot-water canner.

To make specialty vinegars, we steep fresh herbs and other flavorful produce in a variety of vinegars. Experiment with cider, wine or rice vinegars for the interesting flavors they offer.
It is most important to start with a good-quality vinegar especially when using wine vinegars. If herbs are used, bruise or crush them to increase their surface area for maximum flavor extraction during steeping. Most can be made within a week, but allow a little longer for further flavor development.

Serving Suggestions:

To start a meal with pizzazz, garnish a small dish of flavored oil with fresh herbs and serve with pieces of crusty bread for dipping. Be sure to try the Five-Pepper Oil (page 259) on your next pizza. Specialty vinegars dress up tossed greens, pasta and rice salads. Add one of our flavored vinegars to a marinade for less tender meat to get flavor as well as tenderness. A splash of a specialty vinegar or a flavored oil (or both) added to vegetables such as green beans, cauliflower or broccoli is a new eating adventure.

Food Safety Alert

Accurate measurement of the amounts called for in the recipe is essential to making an oil that will not support growth of harmful micro-organisms. If you want a larger quantity of oil than one recipe produces, put a second batch of ingredients (a second recipe) into a separate container. Two containers can be heated at the same time in the oven; just don't put more than 1 cup (250 mL) of oil into one or use a smaller container. When the oil has cooled, it is of the utmost importance to keep the oil refrigerated at all times when it's not in use, and to keep it no longer than 1 month. It is a good idea to check the temperature of your oven with an oven thermometer for accuracy.

List of Recipes: Oils and Vinegars

Flavored Oils

Impress your guests with these wonderful flavored oils. Remember to store in the refrigerator and use within a month.

Basil Oil with Lemon And Black Peppercorns

Oil infused with fresh basil has extraordinary flavor, yet is so simple to make. Serve it in a small bowl with a sprinkling of chopped fresh basil and small pieces of crusty French bread for dipping.

1 cup	canola or extra virgin olive oil	250 mL
6	leaves fresh basil	6
2	strips lemon rind, about ½ x 3 inches (1 x 7.5 cm)	2
8	black peppercorns	8

1. Place oil, basil, lemon rind and peppercorns in a 2-cup (500 mL) glass measuring cup or a 28-oz (796 mL) can that has been washed and dried and had the label removed. Set container on a pie plate. Bake in a 300°F (150°C) oven for 90 minutes or until the basil is blackened and crisp. Remove to a rack to cool for 30 minutes.
2. Line a small strainer with a coffee filter or several layers of cheesecloth. Strain oil into a clean glass jar, cover and store in the refrigerator at all times. Use within a month.

Makes about 1 cup (250 mL).

Five-Pepper Oil

Five peppers team to give amazing flavor to this powerful oil. Be sure to notice that the increased amount of peppers significantly increases the cooking time. The peppers should be blackened and crisp when the oil is finished.

1	small hot red chile pepper	1
1	habañero chile pepper	1
1	small jalapeño pepper	1
¼	sweet red or orange pepper	¼
8	whole black peppercorns	8
1 cup	canola or extra virgin olive oil	250 mL

1. Remove stems from peppers and cut each in half. Place peppers, peppercorns and oil in a 2-cup (500 mL) glass measuring cup or a 28-oz (796 mL) can that has been washed and dried and had the label removed. Set container on a pie plate. Bake in a 300°F (150°C) oven for 4 hours or until the peppers are blackened and crisp. Remove to a rack to cool for 30 minutes.

2. Line a small strainer with a coffee filter or several layers of cheesecloth. Strain oil into a clean glass jar, cover and store in the refrigerator at all times. Use within a month.

Makes about 1 cup (250 mL).

Dried Porcini Mushroom & Rosemary Oil

In Northern Italy, cooks use ingredients that are readily available. So porcini mushrooms and rosemary, which are kitchen basics, and the ever-available olive oil fit this description. A great oil to brush on pizza shells before adding the toppings.

1 cup	extra virgin olive oil	250 mL
¼ cup	dried porcini mushrooms	50 mL
2	sprigs fresh rosemary or 2 tsp (10 mL) dried	2

1. Place oil, mushrooms and rosemary in a 2-cup (500 mL) glass measuring cup or a 28-oz (796 mL) can that has been washed and dried and had the label removed. Set container on a pie plate. Bake in a 300°F (150°C) oven for 1 hour or until the mushrooms are golden brown. Remove to a rack to cool for 30 minutes.

2. Line a small strainer with a coffee filter or several layers of cheese-cloth. Strain oil into a clean jar, cover and store in the refrigerator at all times. Use within a month.

Makes about 1 cup (250 mL).

Oil de Provençe

The flavors of Provençe inspired this excellent and versatile oil. Team it with a mild flavored vinegar when making a salad vinaigrette.

1 cup	canola or extra virgin olive oil	250 mL
2	strips fresh orange rind	
	(about 2½ x 3 inches/1 x 7.5 cm)	2
2	thinly sliced shallots	2
1	bay leaf	1
1 tbsp	chopped fresh thyme leaves or 1 tsp (5 mL) dried	15 mL
1 tsp	fennel seeds	5 mL

1. Place oil, orange rind, shallots, bay leaf, thyme and fennel seeds in a 2-cup (500 mL) glass measuring cup or a 28-oz (796 mL) can that has been washed and dried and had the label removed. Set container on a pie plate.
2. Bake in a 300°F (150°C) oven for 90 minutes or until the shallots are blackened and crisp. Remove to a rack to cool for 30 minutes.
3. Line a small strainer with a coffee filter or several layers of cheesecloth. Strain oil into a clean glass jar, cover and store in the refrigerator. Use within a month.

Makes about 1 cup (250 mL).

Nut-Infused Oils

Authentic nut oils are very expensive, but their ambrosial flavor can be reproduced by the following method. We recommend leaving the nuts in the oil after heating to develop a more intense nut flavor. Although oils made with other flavoring essences must always be strained before storing, nut-infused oils can be stored with the nuts and strained just before use, if desired. We love them in a salad dressing with the nuts providing a nice garnish, either in the mixture or sprinkled on top. No doubt you will find other uses for these exotic oils in your own recipes.

| 1 cup | canola oil | 250 mL |
| ¼ cup | chopped nuts, such as walnuts, pecans or hazelnuts or sliced almonds | 50 mL |

1. Place oil and nuts in a 2-cup (500 mL) glass measuring cup or a 28-oz (796 mL) can that has been washed and dried and had the label removed. Set container on a pie plate.
2. Bake in a 300°F (150°C) oven for 1 hour or until the nuts are dark brown. Remove to a rack to cool for 30 minutes.
3. Pour oil and nuts into a clean glass jar, cover and store in the refrigerator at all times. Use within a month.

Makes about 1 cup (250 mL).

Specialty Vinegars

Once they are made, it is best to use these specialty vinegars within six months since flavor declines during storage.

Fruit Vinegar

Vinegars made with fruit are the most versatile of all the flavored vinegars. Use either fresh or frozen fruit for an ambrosial vinegar.

2 cups	sliced hulled strawberries or 1 cup	
	(250 mL) raspberries, cherries or blueberries	500 mL
½ cup	rice vinegar	125 mL
2 tsp	granulated sugar	10 mL

1. Place fruit in a clean jar. Heat vinegar to boiling, pour over fruit, cover and steep for several days at room temperature, out of direct sunlight.
2. Strain through a fine sieve, pressing to extract liquid; discard pulp. Heat vinegar with sugar until sugar dissolves; pour into a clean jar with a tight-fitting lid. Store in the refrigerator.

Makes 1 cup (250 mL).

Variation:
Mint leaves or tarragon may be added during steeping.

Citron Vinegar

The flavor of citrus adds a bright note to many foods such as fish,
steamed vegetables and vinaigrettes.

1	lime	1
½	orange	½
1	lemon, thinly sliced	1
2 cups	white wine vinegar	500 mL
⅛ tsp	each: salt and paprika	0.5 mL
2 tsp	granulated sugar	10 mL
	strips of lemon rind (optional)	

1. Finely grate rind of lime and orange; combine with lemon slices in
   a saucepan. Squeeze juice from lime and orange; set aside.
2. Add vinegar, salt and paprika to saucepan; bring to a boil over high
   heat, remove from heat and let cool. Stir in reserved juice; pour
   into a clean jar. Cover and steep in a sunny location for 1 week or
   longer.
3. Strain through a fine sieve and discard pulp. Heat vinegar with
   sugar until sugar dissolves; pour into a clean jar with a tight-fitting
   lid. Add lemon rind (if using). Store in the refrigerator.

Makes about 1½ cups (375 mL).

Serving Suggestion:
Creamy Citron Dressing
*One of the neatest ways to use this vinegar is in an oil and vinegar
dressing with crumbled feta cheese.*
Place 2 tbsp (25 mL) crumbled feta cheese, 2 tbsp (25 mL) olive oil,
2 tbsp (25 mL) water, 1 tbsp (15 mL) Citron Vinegar and 1 tbsp (15 mL)
mayonnaise in a blender or food processor; blend until smooth.

Makes ½ cup (125 mL).

Basic Fresh Herb Vinegar

Experiment with various herbs to make flavorful vinegars. Crush or bruise the herbs before adding them for best release of flavor.

2 cups	vinegar	500 mL
	(white wine, red wine, rice, white or cider)	
½ cup	fresh herbs (rosemary, sage, tarragon, thyme, basil, parsley, chives and chive blossoms, mint, dill, oregano) or	
	3 tbsp (45 mL) dried	125 mL

1. Bring vinegar to a boil.
2. Crush or bruise fresh herbs. Place herbs in a clean jar and pour in vinegar. Cover and steep in a sunny location for 2 weeks or longer.
3. Taste vinegar occasionally and when flavor is satisfactory, strain vinegar and pour into a clean jar with a tight-fitting lid. Add a fresh sprig of herb to the jar if desired. Store in the refrigerator.

Makes 2 cups (500 mL).

Suggested Combinations:
Red wine vinegar with sage, oregano or thyme
White wine vinegar with chive blossoms, basil or parsley
Rice vinegar with rosemary
Cider vinegar with tarragon, dill or mint
White wine vinegar with lemon herbs (lemon balm, lemon basil, lemon thyme or lemon verbena)

Cider Sage Vinegar

Sage gives a special flavor to this vinegar; use only the tender stems, discarding the woody ones. Use this vinegar as a glaze for ham or pork. It is also interesting mixed with oil to make a vinaigrette.

2 cups	cider vinegar	500 mL
1	bunch fresh sage leaves	1
3	cinnamon sticks, each 3 inches (8 cm) long	3
½ tsp	whole allspice	2 mL
¼ tsp	whole cloves	1 mL

1. Bring vinegar to a boil. Crush or bruise sage. Half fill a clean pint (500 mL) jar with sage leaves. Add cinnamon sticks, allspice and cloves.
2. Pour vinegar into jar, cover and steep in a sunny location for up to 2 weeks, tasting occasionally.
3. When flavor is satisfactory, strain vinegar and pour into a clean jar with a tight-fitting lid. Add some of the sage leaves and spices, if desired. Store in the refrigerator.

Makes 2 cups (500 mL).

Chile Herb Garlic Vinegar

Garlic vinegars are among our favorites to use for salad dressings and the many dishes where vinegar is added.

2 cups	white wine vinegar	500 mL
3–4	sprigs fresh herb such as basil or thyme	3–4
1	clove garlic, crushed	1
1	hot chile pepper	1

1. Bring vinegar to a boil. Crush or bruise herb. Place herb, garlic and chile in a clean jar.
2. Proceed as in steps 2 and 3 above.

Makes 2 cups (500 mL).

Herbed Lemon Vinegar

We love the fresh flavor of this lemon vinegar. Splash it lightly on fish before baking or use it instead of butter with cooked vegetables. We also use it in a vinaigrette for a fruit salad. Garlic lovers will certainly want to include the garlic!

2	lemons 2	
2 cups	white wine vinegar	500 mL
1 tbsp	dried dill weed, basil, rosemary or tarragon	
	or 4 small sprigs fresh herbs	15 mL
2	cloves garlic, sliced, optional	2
2 tsp	granulated sugar	10 mL

1. Finely grate outside rind of lemons and thinly slice lemons. Combine rind, lemon slices, vinegar, herbs and garlic (if using) in a medium stainless steel or enamel saucepan. Bring to a boil over high heat, remove from heat and let cool.
2. Pour into a clean jar. Cover and steep in a cool dark place for several weeks. Taste vinegar occasionally and when strength is satisfactory, strain vinegar and discard pulp. Heat vinegar with sugar until sugar is dissolved; pour into a clean jar with a tight-fitting lid. Store in the refrigerator.

Makes about 2 cups (500 mL).

Honey Herb Vinegar

The honey gives the vinegar much the same sweetness of balsamic vinegar.

2 cups	**red wine vinegar**	**500 mL**
2 tbsp	**honey**	**25 mL**
½ cup	**fresh thyme or basil leaves**	**125 mL**

1. Bring vinegar to a boil; stir in honey until dissolved.
2. Crush or bruise herbs. Place herbs in a clean jar and pour in vinegar. Cover and steep in a sunny location for 2 weeks or longer, tasting occasionally.
3. When flavor is satisfactory, strain vinegar and pour into a clean jar with a tight-fitting lid. Store in the refrigerator.

Makes 2 cups (500 mL).

Pink Peppercorn Vinegar

The pink peppercorns give a beautiful color to this simple-to-make vinegar. Use both green and pink for a variation.

| 2 cups | white wine vinegar | 500 mL |
| 2 tbsp | pink peppercorns | 25 mL |

Bring vinegar and peppercorns to a boil, reduce heat and boil gently for 5 minutes. Pour into a clean jar with a tight-fitting lid. Steep in a cool, dark place for several weeks. Store in the refrigerator.

Makes 2 cups (500 mL).

Variations:
Pink and Green Peppercorn Vinegar
Use 1 tbsp (15 mL) green and 1 tbsp (15 mL) pink peppercorns.

Tarragon Green Peppercorn Vinegar
Add ½ cup (125 mL) fresh tarragon or 2 tbsp (25 mL) dried.

Provençe-Style Vinegar

This is one of our most popular vinegars. Its delicate flavor is a perfect partner for salads made from young greens. To retain the flavor after bottling, add 2 fresh strips of orange rind, 1 thyme sprig, a slice shallot, 1 bay leaf and a few fennel seeds.

2 cups	white wine vinegar	500 mL
½ cup	fresh thyme leaves	125 mL
5	wide strips orange rind	5
⅓ cup	thinly sliced dried shallots	75 mL
2	bay leaves	2
2 tsp	fennel seeds	10 mL

1. Bring vinegar to a boil. Wash and dry thyme, then crush or bruise. Place thyme, orange strips, shallots, bay leaves and fennel seeds in a clean jar. Pour vinegar into jar, cover and set in a cool, dark place for several weeks.
2. Taste vinegar and when strength is satisfactory, strain it and discard solids. Pour into a clean jar with a tight-fitting lid. Store in the refrigerator.

Makes 2 cups (500 mL).

Red Wine Raspberry Vinegar

The technique used for this recipe produces a more intense fruit flavor than is found in other raspberry vinegars. As a result, you can use it more sparingly. Add a hint of mint by including several sprigs of fresh mint with the raspberries.

2 cups	fresh or frozen raspberries	500 mL
1¼ cups	red wine vinegar	300 mL
⅓ cup	granulated sugar	75 mL
¼ cup	water	50 mL

1. Place raspberries, vinegar, sugar and water in a medium stainless steel or enamel saucepan. Bring to a boil over high heat, reduce heat, cover and boil gently for 5 minutes. Cool before storing; store in the refrigerator overnight.
2. Strain through a fine sieve, pressing to extract liquid; discard pulp. Pour liquid into a clean jar with a tight-fitting lid. Store in the refrigerator.

Makes 2 cups (500 mL).

Red Wine and Rosemary Vinegar

A pungent, colorful vinegar to use for salad dressings or marinades.

2 cups	red wine vinegar	500 mL
1 tsp	granulated sugar	5 mL
½ cup	fresh rosemary leaves	125 mL
½	clove garlic, crushed	½

1. Bring vinegar and sugar to a boil. Crush or bruise rosemary. Place rosemary and garlic in a clean jar and pour in vinegar. Cover and steep in a sunny location for up to 2 weeks, tasting occasionally.
2. When flavor is satisfactory, strain vinegar and pour into a clean jar with a tight-fitting lid. Store in the refrigerator.

Makes 2 cups (500 mL).

Variation:
Cranberry and Rosemary Vinegar
Use white vinegar, omit garlic and add ¼ cup fresh cranberries to jar before pouring in vinegar.

Red Wine Oregano Garlic Vinegar

2 cups	red wine vinegar	500 mL
1 cup	fresh oregano	250 mL
3	cloves garlic, crushed	3

1. Bring vinegar to a boil. Crush or bruise oregano. Place oregano and garlic in a clean jar.
2. Pour vinegar into jar, cover and steep in a sunny location for up to 2 weeks, tasting occasionally. When flavor is satisfactory, strain vinegar and pour into a clean jar with a tight-fitting lid. Store in the refrigerator.

Makes 2 cups (500 mL).

Sherry Vinegar

Sherry vinegar is a superb source of flavor to enliven many foods. Try adding it to hot or cold soups or a simple vinaigrette.

1 cup	white wine vinegar	250 mL
1 cup	sherry	250 mL

Bring vinegar and sherry just to a boil, cool slightly and pour into a clean jar with a tight-fitting lid. Steep in a cool, dark place for several weeks. Store in the refrigerator.

Makes 2 cups (500 mL).

Champagne Vinegar

It is truly exciting to be able to use champagne, the most celebrated of sparkling wines to make a homemade vinegar. So why not celebrate with Champagne Vinegar in a vinaigrette on a salad or splashed over cooked vegetables.

1 cup	dry champagne	250 mL
1 cup	white wine vinegar	250 mL
1 tsp	granulated sugar	5 mL

Bring champagne, vinegar and sugar just to a boil. Remove from heat and cool slightly. Pour into a clean jar with a tight-fitting lid. Steep in a cool, dark place for several weeks. Store in the refrigerator.

Makes 2 cups (500 mL).

Vinaigrettes and Dressings

Now that we have talked about specialty vinegars and flavored oils, here are some of our favorite ways to use them.

Light Garlic Basil Vinaigrette

Use this dressing on a salad of tossed greens or mesclun, to marinate meats or to sprinkle on steamed vegetables for a vegetable salad.

¼ cup	chicken broth	50 mL
3 tbsp	Basil Oil with Lemon and Black Peppercorns (page 249)	45 mL
1 tbsp	red wine vinegar	15 mL
2 tsp	lemon juice	10 mL
1 tsp	Dijon-Style Mustard (page 232)	5 mL
1	clove garlic, crushed	1
1 tbsp	chopped fresh basil or 1 tsp (5 mL) dried	15 mL

Combine all ingredients in a small container with a tight-fitting lid. Cover and shake well. Refrigerate until ready to use.

Makes ½ cup (125 mL).

Oregano Pepper Vinaigrette

This is a robust vinaigrette. It delivers zip to many an ordinary green salad. Drizzle some on sliced tomatoes. We like it with a pasta salad.

⅓ cup	Five-Pepper Oil (page 259)	75 mL
¼ cup	dry red wine	50 mL
1 tbsp	chopped fresh oregano or 1 tsp (5 mL) dried	15 mL
1 tbsp	red wine vinegar	15 mL
1	clove garlic, crushed	1
¼ tsp	salt	1 mL

Combine all ingredients in a small container with a tight-fitting lid. Cover and shake well. Refrigerate until ready to use.

Makes about ½ cup (125 mL).

Serving Suggestion:
Greek Salad
Place 8 cups (2 L) torn romaine lettuce, ½ red onion and ½ English cucumber, thinly sliced, ¼ cup (50 mL) pitted kalamata olives, 2 medium tomatoes cut into wedges and ½ cup (125 mL) crumbled feta cheese in a large bowl. Pour Oregano Pepper Vinaigrette over salad; toss well.

Makes 8 servings.

Raspberry Orange Vinaigrette

This is the perfect vinaigrette to use with fruit salads and with cottage cheese salads. And use it as a marinade for chicken and pork before grilling.

⅓ cup	orange juice	75 mL
¼ cup	each: extra virgin olive oil and water	50 mL
2 tbsp	Red Wine Raspberry Vinegar (page 272)	25 mL
1	chopped green onion	1
⅛ tsp	each: salt and freshly ground pepper	0.5 mL

Combine all ingredients in a small container with a tight-fitting lid. Cover and shake well. Refrigerate until ready to use.

Makes ⅔ cup (150 mL).

Creamy Champagne Dressing

You don't need to wait for a special day to make this flavorful dressing using our Champagne Vinegar. Use it for salads of shredded cabbage, chopped celery and diced apple, or for a light potato salad.

3 tbsp	light mayonnaise	45 mL
3 tbsp	Champagne Vinegar (page 275)	45 mL
2 tbsp	canola oil	25 mL
1 tbsp	chopped fresh parsley	15 mL
1 tbsp	water	15 mL
1 tsp	Old-Style Whole Seed Mustard or coarse mustard	5 mL

Whisk together mayonnaise, vinegar, oil, parsley, water and mustard in a small bowl. Transfer to a container with a tight-fitting lid. Cover and refrigerate until ready to use.

Makes about ½ cup (125 mL).

tip

Mesclun: Today there is much consumer interest in a variety of lettuces usually called mesclun or mixed young salad greens. They are available in almost every produce store and supermarket, sold by weight. Typically they are a combination of mild- and bitter-flavored tender young leaves of different colors. The combination usually includes oak leaf and red leaf lettuces, frisée (curly endive), mâche and radicchio, and may include spinach, red mustard, arugula and others. Store as you would other greens and use as soon as possible, ideally within a couple of days.

INDEX